CW01304595

So What Can I Do?

Answers from Inspired Researchers about the World Today

So What Can I Do?

Answers from Inspired Researchers about the World Today

Kim Kamala Ekman
Editor

Copyright, 2017 by Kim Kamala Ekman

All rights exclusively reserved. No part of this book may be reproduced or translated into any language or utilized in any form or by any means, electronic or mechanical, including photocopying, recording or by any information storage and retrieval system, without permission in writing from the publisher.

So What Can I Do? ISBN 978-1522711261 Hard Copy Soft Cover Book
2nd Edition

Cover design and layout by Kim Kamala Ekman / Ole Dammegård

Disclaimer and Reader Agreement

Under no circumstances will the publisher, Kim Kamala Ekman, be liable to any person or business entity for any direct, indirect, special, incidental, consequential, or other damages based on any use of this book or any other source to which it refers, including, without limitation, any lost profits, business interruption, or loss of programs or information.

Reader Agreement for Accessing This Book

By reading this book, you, the reader, consent to bear sole responsibility for your own decisions to use or read any of this book's material. Kim Kamala Ekman shall not be liable for any damages or costs of any type arising out of any action taken by you or others based upon reliance on any materials in this book.

CONTENTS

Acknowledgements — *8*

Preface — *9*

Max Igan — *15*

David Icke — *35*

Kerry Cassidy — *89*

Ole Dammegård — *119*

Kevin Barrett — *149*

Sofia Smallstorm — *177*

Zen Gardner — *195*

Cynthia McKinney — *219*

Acknowledgement

I wish to express my gratitude to the following people for their help and support in creating this book:

* To Ole Dammegård, my soul mate and rock in life. Thank you for helping to design the book cover and for your endless patience, time and support.

* Thank you Zen Gardner, for being a light and inspiration when this idea came to me.

* Thank you Louise Sutton, for helping with the questions.

* Thank you Åsa Ekman, my sister who always gives me straight forward feedback, good ideas and for proof reading the Swedish translation.

* Thank you very much Tom Kimball, for proof reading and for being extremely efficient during this process.

* Thank you very much Evert Wängberg, for translating the book to Swedish.

PREFACE

Why is every country and everyone in debt?
Are we living in collective insanity?
Can we save ourselves and the world, and if so, how?
With the scientific knowledge of today, why are there so much disease?
Do we have free choice?
Are we living an inversion?
Who can we trust?
...And what can I do?....

If you in any way doubt the government, the banks, or the system we live in today, please continue reading. You will be blown away by the information from these brilliant researchers and their answers about the world today. With this knowledge you will be more aware of what is going on behind the scenes and what you can do about it.

I admire every one that I have interviewed for this book and their dedication, courage and huge hearts. I thank them all from the bottom of my heart for taking the time to answer the questions and help make this book come alive to serve for the better of this world.

I believe that we can't do much without awareness and knowledge.

If you have never been interested in knowing why politicians, big corporations, the banks and others are running the world the way they are, but feel an urge for straightforward truth and change, this book is a great start.

You will get a clearer view of very profound information in an easy-to-understand format from amazingly knowledgeable people that have been working in their fields for many, many years.

Since my teens I have always had a gut feeling that the system we live in is far from transparent and true, not working for the people, but rather for the very few in control at the top of the pyramid.

In 1997 David Ickes's book, The Robot's Rebellion, landed in my lap. I was so grateful, finally, that somebody wrote with meaning and truth about what the world really is like. I wanted to share this with my family, friends, well the whole world, but no one was interested. I felt very lonely, confused and frustrated and I see that in many others today. How was it possible that no one wanted to tap into the truth and explore different researchers that I had started to find and learn from?

I know for a fact that there are many people out there who are feeling the same way I did, not trusting the media, politicians, the system, the pharmaceutical industry etc. anymore, and maybe feeling that there is nothing you can do, or you might be stuck in the economic slavery of mortgages and debts, or have lost trust in the future.

Well, good news, there are loads of things you can do on a daily basis to change your own world and the one around you for the better and help each other to step out from this darkness.

It might shake your world, but it will be worth it, big time. Our heart knows the truth, and stepping into the truth will lead us to many new different paths. Beautiful doors will open along the way. Like-minded people will start coming your way. Now is the time for all of us to connect, without revenge or hatred in our hearts.

I invite you to be brave and get informed. Do you dare?

Together we can and will make a change for the better, for all.

Never forget: you are not alone.

Kim Kamala Ekman

A mind that is stretched to a new experience can never go back to its old dimension.

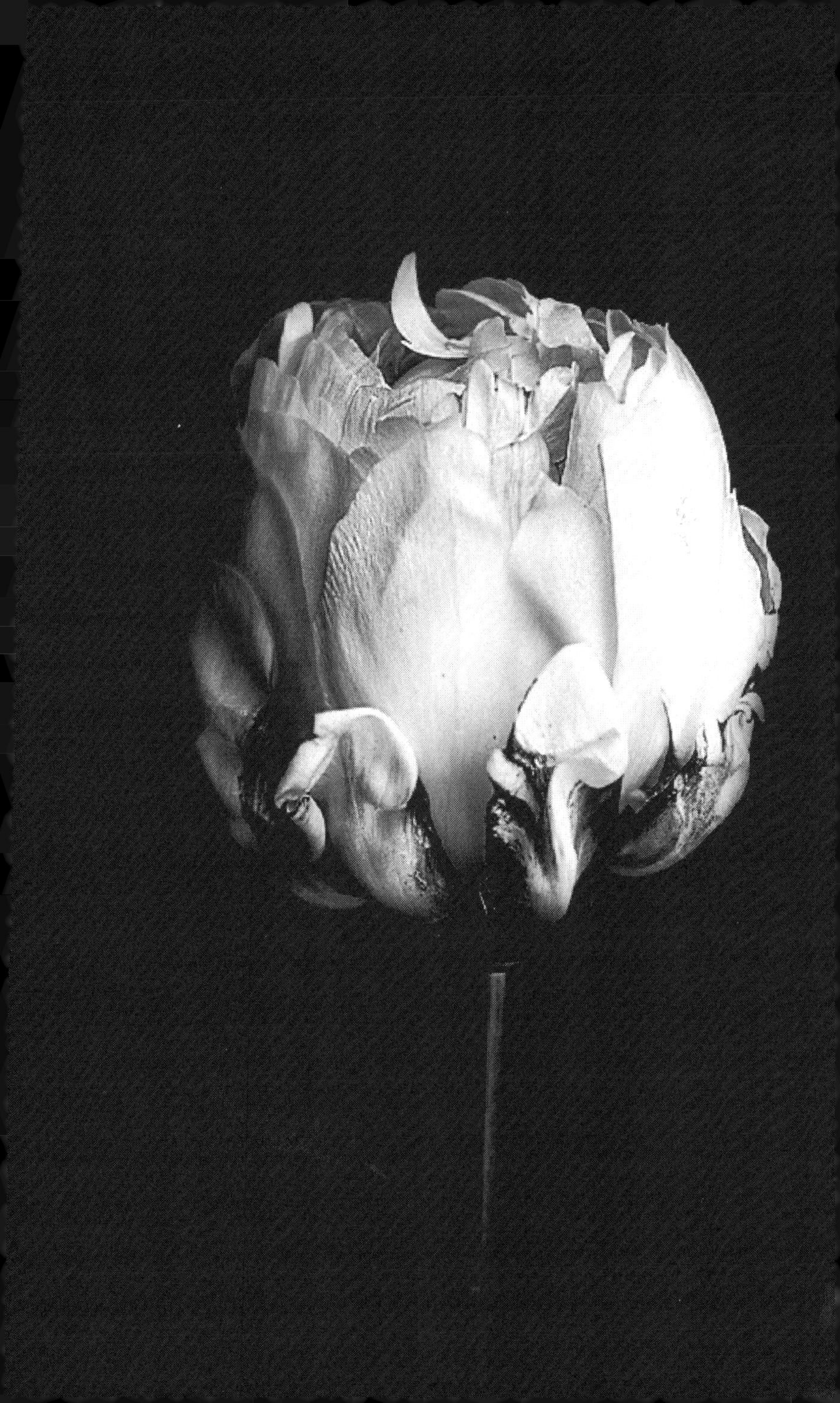

MAX IGAN

MAX IGAN

Introduction

Max Igan is a researcher, truth seeker, radio host, international speaker, film-maker and one of the leaders of the global awakening movement. This man is a must-listen-to for all those serious about stopping the NWO in its tracks.

The most famous films of Max Igan (especially among those involved in truth movement) are The Awakening (2008), The Calling (2009) and Trance-Formation (2012) which have been widely acclaimed and watched by well over one million viewers worldwide.

www.thecrowhouse.com

When did you start exploring your field, was there a specific event that led you to this path the waking up?

I've actually been on this path pretty well my whole life. I woke up to the fact that something was terribly wrong when I was four years old when I found out that people had to buy land. I couldn't comprehend that, I couldn't understand how people could feel that they could own part of the Earth. And how government figured they owned it and we had to purchase it off the government. I just couldn't knock this out when I was four years old. It really, really disturbed me.

So I looked at the world from a different perspective from that point from a wonder size and when I was eight years old I discovered the pyramids. And my mother told me that no one knew how they were built and so I put down all the Batman comics and wanted to find out how the pyramids were built. So it started very young for me. So when I was about eight years old I started to research the pyramids and gave up on the Batman comics and I wanted to know how we got here.

I started really looking into history. I started reading encyclopedias and got a real fascination with ancient history. When you start looking at ancient history, you start to realize that it's very different from what they have told us. And if you really go further down that rabbit hole, you begin to start to question, well why wouldn't they tell us this? I started to think, well this is a cover up of some sort, so why is there a cover up. Then of course you get into why the government does the things it does and you realize that there's a massive cover up in virtually every aspect of our lives and most people are living in a dream world. This is why I obviously felt so uncomfortable when I was four.

But whatever it is that gets you into it, for me it was ancient history. For many people it could be U.F.O.'s, it could be whatever, but eventually it leads to the point where you start to understand that there is a major cover up of every aspect of our society. There are very deep and dark things going on behind the scenes. You start looking into that and the rabbit hole goes very deep.

How do you see the world today in the terms of the challenges facing us?

I see us walking on a knife-edge at the moment. Humanity is in a very, very poignant place in history, a very important place in history, and we have the potential to go either way. The powers that be believe they are in the midst of a massive attempt to lock us down. But there is a great awakening happening. Unfortunately not quick enough. A lot of people are half awake, but too many people are locked in their own rabbit holes and locked in their own belief systems and looking for someone to point a finger at. And they're not really prepared to look behind the scenes and see what is really causing this and where the shadows and darkness really comes from. We have been given a lot of different things to investigate if you really go down looking at the cover ups and everything I was talking about before. You start looking down these rabbit holes and you can find enough information to point the finger at anybody you want, Zionism, or Judaism, or the Vatican system, the Jesuit system, or the freemasons, or whoever you want.

You can mount enough evidence to raise a reasonable case to any of these entities. But what you need to realize is that all of them are connected and it is what sits behind that that is the real problem. What sits behind that is really an occult system and a cult society. It's almost like a shadow society that sits behind our society that is, for want of a better word, farming this society. The society that we see on the surface is essentially being founded by those who sit behind the scenes. They keep the people in the world in a state of debt slavery, always running on the treadmill, so they don't have too much time to look around to see what's going on.

Behind that is an occult system that is basically farming and harvesting the human race in a variety of ways. It's whether people are going to wake up to what's really going on and embrace the mechanism that will be required to step out of this situation. There are too many people who are looking for a leader, someone to come up with a grand plan to lead us to safety. They're not realizing that people have to do it themselves. People have to readjust their moral compass and apply that to the world that they live in and realize that they don't have to abide by any rule or anything that claims to be law, which is causing them to step outside the sphere of their moral compass.

Of course the hardest part in this is getting to the order-followers, getting the order-followers — the police, the military — to realize that they don't have to carry out orders that are causing them to step outside the sphere of their moral compass. The problem is that on many of the higher echelons of the groups of our society — whether it is politics, whether it is military, whether it's the law enforcement, the religious aspects, education — you find that the higher echelons of all of these organizations, are all part of this shadow society and so dictate the rules to those below them.

So we're at a really pivotal point. There's a lot of stuff going on in the world today that is causing people to look around them, and the blinkers are falling off. But again it's quite frightening for a lot of people, because if you're new to this information or when it reveals itself to you, and it's revealing itself very dramatically recently, it can be very frightening to people and very confronting to people, and that's one of the problems. Fortunately there is a reasonable amount of people in the independent media who are providing a safety net for those who are waking up. And hopefully they will look for the right source in there and find their way through.

Does it matter if we vote or not?

Well, this is an interesting question. You know it depends on the system that we live in, it depends on the country that you live in as whether voting was going to make a difference. In the case of the United States in some ways it's important to vote, because there is an opportunity, there is a chance that someone like yourself with enough support could be propelled to the right position. Whether they get assassinated on the way is another question, because the system is so rigged.

But then again in countries such as Australia where it's compulsory to vote and you're only given basically two or three parties to vote for and they're all completely compromised. In this sort of a situation, it's best if people don't vote.

Like in Australia all I can see is a massive boycott of all elections, everyone should stay home that day and say, there are no suitable candidates. The problem with the United States system of course is that if everybody does that, then the criminals still vote. And with the United States system, it doesn't matter if any one hundred people vote. If those hundred people vote for Hillary Clinton, then Hillary Clinton is president. That's the way it goes. It depends on the country that you are living in. Ultimately my surviving systems are compromised. But even with what we've just seen in the United States, there was just such a massive landslide towards Donald Trump that they couldn't cover it up. So you know in that sort of a situation, it can make a difference. It just depends on the country that you're in and the political system they got installed.

What are your thoughts about money and the global banks?

Money is an interesting thing and money is something that we all use. But it's something that people really don't like to talk about, because it's so confusing for them. Money could be a great tool for us just to perform commerce with, but the current monetary system that we've got at the moment is designed to create scarcity. It's designed to place people in a state of debt slavery and keep them running on the treadmill for their entire life. They are paying off debts that can never ever be paid off, and they're even constructing it and reinforcing it in such a way that these debts will hopefully be passed on to your children. That's what they're hoping for, anyway.

So it's disgraceful the money system that we've got. It's something that people take for granted, something that people use every day, but they never ask where it comes from. If people understood the injustice of the money system as was once said by one president of the United States, there would be a revolution before morning. That is the state of the global monetary system. It's designed to create scarcity, to create competition, and to basically milk the resources of this planet. If it follows its natural course of permanent growth, it will succeed in changing this planet into a rubbish dump and discarding the entire human race, and that's its purpose.

What do you think about the debt-based economy people are stuck in? Is there a way out?

Well, the way out is to introduce an honest monetary system and this reflects on the last question. It is a completely debt-based society, that's how money is created. It's created through debt. So anything would be better than what we've got. The interesting thing about money is that once you introduce it into a person's mind, it becomes very difficult for that person to think in terms without money. If you go to a tribal culture that never used currency and you introduce a form of currency to these people, within a year or two they wouldn't know how to live without it. So it's an interesting thing.

But the system of debt-based currency that we've got at the moment, the only way maybe is to go back to a gold standard. Yeah, that might work, but then who's got all the gold at the moment? It certainly isn't you or me, it's the rich people that have all the gold. If we go back to a gold standard, there is a chance that the people who run the system are going to hold all the cards right from the very beginning and it's going to end up back where we were.

Something like tally sticks would work. We had tally sticks for decades and possibly even centuries and it was no problems with things like that. I mean currency, money is simply something that we use to perform commerce and it could be something that society can benefit from and simply makes society work easier.

But I think it's the whole economic basis of society that is the problem, our propensity to think of society in economic terms and to think of life and resources and trees and grass and everything in economic terms. Even when there is a fire or a disaster, we say well there was twelve billion dollars' worth of damage. What about the life? What about the life value of the damage? Why does it have to have a monetary value? Why do we think in economic terms? So really I would like to see a world without money. But I think it would be an interesting shift for people to have to go through, that would have to be a lot of reeducation of how people think for that to happen.

We have started to read and hear about micro-chipping people. What does that mean?

All micro-chipping is so dangerous and so much of an affront against your privacy. Micro-chipping is essentially putting a back door into the biological computer that is your body, which is magnetically based. It's possible to do just about anything with these microchips. Also it's leading towards a cashless society and a society where everything that you say and do can be on your microchip. You can open your door, you can open your condo, or you can start your car, you can access your bank, your passport. It's all in the microchip that's been implanted within you.

It could be very convenient, but the problem with it is that if you start speaking out against the government if the government wants to do something that you don't like and you start making noises to point out the criminality, then all they have to do is turn off your microchip and call you a dissident and suddenly you can't open your house door, you can't access your bank account all of your possessions become basically virtual, all access to your possessions now belongs to the virtual world.

So that can be turned on and off at any time, anytime the government chooses to do so. And when you look at the track record of these governments, this is a pretty good control system to be putting in place. The potential for abuse of micro-chipping in this type of control system should make anybody think not twice, not three times, but four or five or six times, many times before ever, ever doing this. I would suggest that no one ever, ever get micro-chipped. It is one of the most dangerous proposals that have ever been presented.

What are your thoughts about depopulation?

Depopulation is happening all around us every day as we speak. You know it's happening in so many subtle ways, it's not just happening through the wars and the obviously population missing in the Middle Eastern countries, through the starvation of Africa. It's also happening in our own countries. It's happening by the marginalization of different countries.

But it's happening in our own countries via poverty and by GMO foods and all things they are introducing to us to lower the human experience. The banning of cannabis is something that lots of people don't even want to talk about, but cannabis is a very medicinal plant and when they outlawed it, we started developing major health problems. Then the pharmaceutical industry stepped in and has been feeding us drugs. It's actually shortened the human life span dramatically.

But when you look at the economic model and you start raising the cost of living and you start discarding more and more people along the way, they become homeless, they end up in the privatized prisons. It all leads to depopulation. It's all part of the same agenda. Depopulation is happening on this earth on a massive scale.

It's being carried out on a massive front, a massive amount of different fronts. And it's happening in ways that people really don't notice, because it's very, very subtle. It's very often soft-kill operations such as the toxins they put in the food, again which will get closer to getting sick, getting into slavery to the medical industry so they can milk your wealth the whole time that they are feeding you drugs and all these things for all these illnesses you're getting from all the stuff they're putting in the food and the fluoride in the water. There are so many ways this is being carried out.

But it is definitely an ongoing thing. It's definitely policy from most governments, if not all governments, and it's definitely happening all around us. If people would simply take the blinkers off and look around them and ask are why their lives the way they are? Ask why the world is in the state that it's in? Because it's happening all around us, not just in countries that are marginalized, but it's happening around in our own community every day.

What is your opinion on vaccines? And are vaccinations parts of the depopulation question?

Absolutely, I think it is part of the depopulation question. Vaccination totally compromises people's immune systems. If you look at studies, you'll find that children that are unvaccinated are far less likely to get ill. They are far less susceptible to diseases than people who are vaccinated. Again this messes up your immune system and get you subservient to the pharmaceutical industry. So it's all the same thing. It also sets up different biological environments within people, changes the genetic environment within people, experimentation, and transhumanism.

You can tie all of this in with some of the aerial spraying the goes on. This is another topic that people don't really want to look at. But there is a lot of aerial spraying going on and we are finding all sorts of agents coming down in the air. Red blood cells, all sorts of things, microscopic agents that we are finding in the sky, in the rocks, in the soil and in the water. So it's happening on a massive scale. It's almost like part of a genetic engineering program it's almost like human biology is being changed on the inside out. I suspect that vaccination has something to do with that. But there's certainly nothing healthy in vaccination.

Even when you look at the charts for vaccination, if you look at things such as smallpox, look at things such as polio, go and get the charts that go back three or four hundred years ago, you find that all of these diseases where on their way out, when the vaccinations were introduced. The vaccinations did not stop the spread of these diseases; these diseases were naturally dying out anyway. And there are a lot of diseases that can be seen to be spreading via vaccinations. There have been several instances in Africa where they've been seeing infected people; vaccinations have been causing all sorts of diseases. So yeah, this is definitely part of the depopulation agenda.

You can even look at Bill Gates; he said that we could lower the global population with a good vaccination agenda. They even tell you what they're doing.

What are GMOs?

GMOs are genetically modified organisms. This is when the government and various institutions start modifying our food to improve profits in commerce. What you find that they are doing is they're inserting all sorts of different genes into vegetables and all sorts of stuff like this. They are putting fish genes and potatoes and monkey genes in tomatoes and all sorts of stuff like this very, very bizarre stuff.

When you look at GMO food, you'll find that you' feed it to an animal, the animal wont eat it, unless there is absolutely no other choice. Look at artificial sweetness in sweets and lollies and candy you buy at the store. If you drop one on the sidewalk, the ants won't eat it, the ants walk around it. Nothing will eat this food. So something is terribly wrong with this food.

When you look at studies that they have done with GMO food on all species, mainly rats, but they have done it on a lot of species. When you feed GMO food to rats for three generations, in the second generation, they start developing genitalia malformations and by the third generation, there are unable to breed. So it takes three generations to see the effect of food, it takes three generations to see the effect on organisms, so what you're going to find is that after three generations of eating GMO food, then people are having trouble breeding.

When you look now, you find a lot of people are having trouble getting pregnant. A lot of young couples are having trouble having children. And this is just an ongoing thing, again back to the depopulation agenda. This is how they do it by changing our genetics from the inside out. God made food the way it is supposed to be. Us messing with food, putting fish genes into potatoes and monkey genes into tomatoes does not make us smart people. It's not a good thing to do. It's not good for the organism.

Even when you look at things such as mad cow disease they started messing around with the food they were feeding the cows. When you start messing around with the food and you start changing the genetic structure of the food and you start feeding it to anybody, then we start taking on the genetic characteristics of that food. And it's very, very dangerous and a lot of GMO food has been banned in a lot of countries in Europe, banned in a lot of countries in South America. GMO food should be labeled, it should be investigated. We should really look at this. It's doing an enormous amount of damage to human biology and people should stay away from it as much as they can.

Do chemtrails exist? If so, how would you describe them?

Chemtrails do exist. They've been classified as or declassified by many governments. In the United States they call it geoengineering, in England a few years ago in the House of Commons they documented the climate remediation program that they're undertaking. It is confirmed that they are spraying. You just got to look at the sky. You can see it. This didn't happen when I was a child. Planes did not have big long exhausts like this. Chemtrails are very different from contrails. Contrails are condensation formed when the hot air of the jet mixes with the cold air, the cold atmosphere, and ice particles are formed. But of course ice is heavier than air, so the ice falls quickly into the warmer air and it dissipates. Contrails naturally dissipate, because they're ice particles which are heavier than air condensation.

That's the way it works. Anything that lingers in the sky is not a normal contrail, it's a spray. It's some sort of agent that's been put in the sky. People from Karnik institute have done tests, a lot of people have done tests on this stuff, tests on the water samples, and soil samples, and they are finding all sorts of bizarre things in there. We're finding barium, strontium, and nanotechnology in the chemtrails. Morgellons syndrome is a lot of stuff that is being attributed to these chemtrails.

But it is absolutely happening, but it appears to be a multi-platform delivery system. We've found broken red blood cells. What are they doing floating around in the sky? We found all sorts of stuff barium, strontium, aluminum as I said earlier. Massive amount of aluminum which is affecting the soil, affecting the crops, people are having a hard time growing their food, people's vegetable gardens are dying, a lot of the trees are dying around the place. Again, part of the depopulation agenda.

Chemtrails can be used to deliver all sorts of things. There's a film that was released a few years ago by a man called Ray Kurzweil, who talked about infusing everything on earth with nanotechnology. He said that soon everything will be fused with nanotechnology, the rocks, the trees, everything. Well, if this is the plan, what sort of delivery system would you use? Aerial spraying would be the perfect delivery system to blanket the world with nanotechnology and certain biological agents that you wanted to put out there, to achieve your agenda whatever that agenda might be, which we're still attempting to uncover.

But yes, chemtrails are certainly happening. There is most certainly aerial spraying going on. And it's one of the most obvious and yet one of the most denied things that you can see around you every day.

Please share your thoughts about the environment and the current weather conditions.

The current weather conditions are a result of a lot of the aerial spraying that we are seeing. But I don't believe in global warming, I don't believe in climate change as it's put to us. But if you go back many years, you'll find that medieval weather was a lot warmer than it is now. I don't really believe anything that we are being fed about the climate. I think that there's a lot going on to make it all seem like it's bad. Perhaps this is partly because of the chemtrails and partly aerial spraying. But it's not nearly so bad as what we are being told. We are not destroying the earth. If we stop the aerial spraying, stop some of the pollution, and stop the wars, then we'll see things fix itself up pretty quickly.

I think the blue skies will come back once they stop the spraying. I don't really see any problem with the climate. We're being fed propaganda in that respect.

Do you have a practice that keeps your spirit high?

Well, just knowing what life is really. I don't have any stake in the outcome of this ride, I'm here of a blink of an eye or breath. Everybody is. What's important about a life is what you do with the time that you've got here. Thinking that you have a stake in the outcome, I mean anything you do here you can't take with you. Anything you collect you can't take with you. I just put things in motion and see where they go. If the human race destroys itself, it's not my fault. I did the best I could to point out that there was another way.

But my life here is a temporary thing, it's a temporary existence. I came here ultimately to die. It's what I do with the information that I get, how I share that information and what I do with the experience along the way. Knowing what life is, knowing that it's an energy universe. Knowing that I am connected to all that is and knowing that even one single thought, if it reaches the right mind, it can make a difference. Just putting that stuff out there and being who I am, living my life is an artistic expression of correction and knowing I have no owners regardless of what anybody says or thinks. And knowing that it's all about the experience. To me that keeps me going you know.

Sometimes there are dark moments, but ultimately it's just about the experience, it's about the journey, and I don't have a stake in the outcome of any of this and that probably keeps me going, keeps me balanced anyway.

Seeing the madness around me I feel hopeless. Can you suggest some ways that would help me regain my trust in the future, and how to act to make positive change?

Well, what you've got to do is be a shining light in all that you do and lead by example in all that you do. Help as many people around you as you can. You can form collection groups and start getting involved in your community, start inspiring them. But even when you're bringing this type of information to people, don't be a merging of doom, be someone who is pleasurable to be around, inspire people with your knowledge, inspire people to want to have the information that you've got. Because they can see how positive you are.

You know we can make a better future, we really can. But we've got to be prepared to face the shadows that exist beyond the vale. The unfortunate thing is most people won't face the shadows in themselves and so they don't believe that shadows exist in other people. Don't believe that people could be capable of the darkness that we see in the world in the real darkness the goes on in this cult world that exists behind system. People are capable of that, but we can change it by simply stepping into the sphere of our moral compass and leading by example in all that we do.

To me that has made a real difference in my life. I give a lot to people, but I don't allow myself to be taken from. There's a difference. There're people who just want you to give them stuff all the time. But there are situations where you can give and you can change a life and that life could go on to change other lives. Seeing these moments is really important.

And getting involved in your community and questioning authority. Asking why anyone has the right to exercise a right of ownership over you. No one has the right to own anybody else. Slavery is illegal in the world. Slavery is abominable. No one that has the right to be Massa over anybody. No one should be a slave to anybody else. What we have now is a system of slavery, a system of debt slavery. Government is basically racketeering. It's extortion. It's protection over money. They say walk between the lines, if you don't walk between the lines, we will take you and put you in a cage. That's extortion.

We can point to a start to a local community by leading by example in what we do. And if we get strength of numbers we can stand up and question the system. Just stand up for yourselves, step into your power, know that everything on this earth that we're dealing with it comes from humans, it's people here. Nobody has any more value than anybody else. Just knowing that in yourself, will make a real difference.

If you could plant one seed in the mainstream mind, what would that be?

Well, almost everything that I just said: knowing what you are. Understanding that you're being lied to by the system. You are powerful. There's a whole world out there and it's not the world that television is telling you about. If I could plant a seed in the mainstream, it would be integrity. It would be the need for people to identify their moral compass and always operate within the sphere of their moral compass and question any law, any legislation, any command that comes from anybody, that causes them to step outside the sphere of their moral compass. Integrity has no need of rules. It doesn't. If we do the right thing in all that we do, all the time, then the world has to change around us.

We don't even have to create a new system, the system has to change around us if we stop following orders, which cause us to step outside the sphere of our moral compass. That's the seed I would plant in people's minds. To examine which way your moral compass points and make sure you always follow it, regardless of anything anybody suggests otherwise.

Seek the truth or hide your head in the sand. Both require digging.

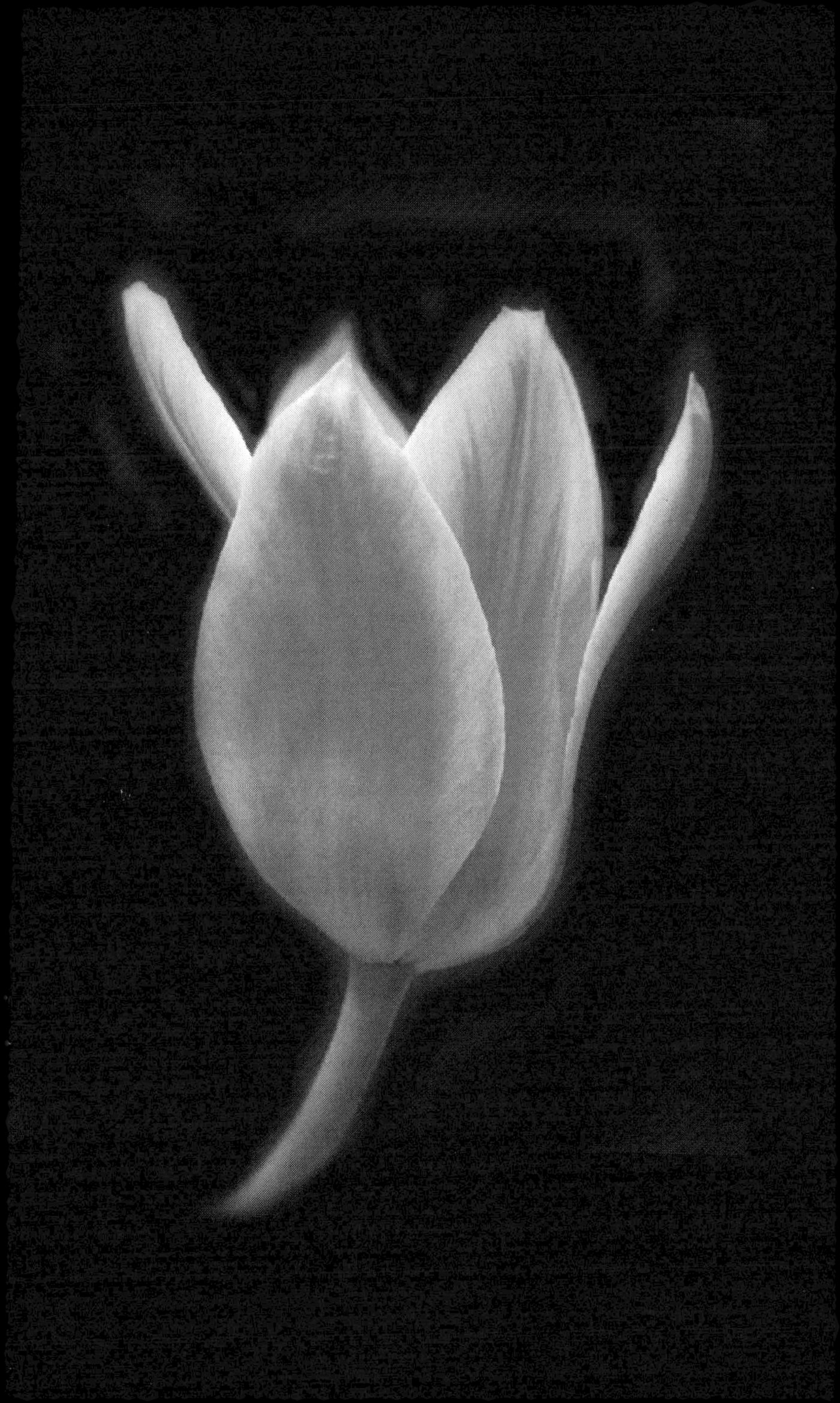

DAVID ICKE

David Icke

DAVID ICKE

Introduction

David Vaughan Icke is an English writer, public speaker, and former media personality best known for his views on what he calls "who and what is really controlling the world". Describing himself as the most controversial speaker and author in the world, he has written many books explaining his position, dubbed "New Age conspiracism", and has attracted a substantial following across the political spectrum.

David has travelled to more than 50 countries researching and talking at public events, like Wembley arena in London where he held the attention of close to 12,000 people for ten hours. And, as the world takes ever more blatantly the form that he describes in his books, the interest in his work has exploded. He hope that he have shown people that, no matter how bad and hopeless things may look, you can survive and prosper if you are prepared to keep walking in your chosen direction and never give up.

His words are designed to inspire all of us to be who we really are, to fling open the door of the mental prison we build for ourselves and to walk into the light of freedom. His example is one we can all appreciate, learn from, and emulate as we break out of the "bubble" that has kept us imprisoned for so long.

www.davidicke.com

When did you start exploring your field? Was there a specific event that led you to this path about waking up?

Oh yes, very much so. I was a presenter with the BBC, presenter of sport and news on BBC television out of London. And I had also started to get involved in green politics , because I saw the world that I grew up in being concreted over and many environmentally unpleasant things being done.

And my life being an extraordinary series of synchronicities, in the sense that I became a professional footballer which I wanted to be from when I was a kid. And the synchronistic sequence of events that led me to being a footballer was extraordinary in itself. Then I had a professional football career until I was twenty-one, which I had to finish with because of arthritis.

Then again, there was a synchronistic series of events that led to me being a newspaper journalist, a radio journalist, eventually a television journalist, and then becoming a green politician for a time. These apparently unconnected professions I later understood were links in a chain. Because the emotional strengths that losing the football career I dreamed about from when I was a kid, gave me emotional strength.

The media career in newspapers and radio and television, showed me how the media works and how the media is not a vehicle for telling people what is happening in the world... but for telling people what the system, the establishment, if you like, is what wants people to think is going on in the world.

Then I got into green politics and that gave me the insight to see how politics works and it's a very horrible sight, I can tell you. Even the Green Party in Britain kind of just fell into the same program. And

David Icke

I think during this chat the word program is going to come up a lot. Then while I was still in green politics, I was a national spokesman for the British Green Party and I was still working for the BBC as a presenter.

Some very strange things started to happen to me during 1989. When I was in a room alone, it was like I wasn't alone. That there was a presence there, but there was nothing you could see. But it was something you could feel. This went on and on for a year and got more and more powerful... more and more tangible... until in early 1990.

I was sitting on a bed in a hotel room in London working for the BBC in the room alone. And this presence was so powerful... so there... that I said out loud, "If there's something there, someone there, would you please contact me, because your driving me up the wall?" A few days later, maybe just slightly more than a few days, but not long, I was at a bookshop on the Isle of Wight, just ten minutes from where I'm sitting now, off the south coast of England. I was with my son, Gareth, who's a big strapping guy now, but was a little boy then, and someone stopped me.

We're on the seafront here and someone stopped me, a railway worker talking about football, because that's what I was presenting among other things for the BBC. After this little chat, I realised that Gareth was no longer there. But I knew where he would be, he'll be in this bookshop newsagent on the seafront. I went in to say to him, "Come on, we'll get off and go into town," I said to my son. And as I looked at him he was reading a book, and as I went to turn to go out, it was like my feet were stuck to the ground. The feeling was like magnets pulling my feet to the floor, and because I'm standing there completely bewildered. I'd come across nothing like this before, nothing like this had ever happened to me before.

At this point where I'm trying to work out what's going on. I wouldn't say it was a voice... it was more like a very strong thought form went through my mind. And it said, "Go look at the books on the far side." And of course in my bewilderment with all this going on, it's like, "What is happening?"

David Icke

So I started to walk towards these books. I knew this newsagent very well, it's still there. I knew that the books were basically romantic novels for the tourists, because this is a seaside town that I live in. I walked across, and in among the romantic novels was this book with a woman's face on it. I was attracted to it, because it was different first of all, and picked it up, and it was called, Mind to Mind. I turned it over and I looked at the blurb on the back and I saw the word psychic. It was a life story of the psychic, Betty Shine.

As soon as I saw the word psychic I got interested, because my immediate thought standing there with a book in my hand was, I wonder if this woman would be able to pick up what I've been feeling around me for the last year. So I took it out and I read it in a day and I contacted her and went to see her. She's off near a place called Brighton... not too far from me... and I went to see her the first time. What I said to her was I've got arthritis which is what ended my football career. I wonder if your hand on healing, which is what she also did, would maybe help.

Part of me was interested in that. But the real reason was, "Will she pick this up." Of course I wasn't going to tell her anything what was happening to me, because that would be ridiculous. So I turn up the first time, I get the hands on healing, had a nice chat. The second time and then the third time, I'm lying on this kind of medical bench couch in her front room. She's doing sort of hands on healing near my left knee. And suddenly I felt like a spider's web on my face. And what struck me immediately was that's what I had read in a book, which she said that when other levels of reality... whatever you want to call them...other realities of existence... entities... are trying to lock into you, it sometimes feels like a spider web on your face.

Now of course what I didn't know then, but what I know now is what that feeling was. It was electromagnetic energy. There was an electromagnetic connection being made into that room, and this is the kind of the same kind of energy you get when you are in a big sports stadium and everyone's excited and people say 'all of the hairs on the back of my neck stood up.' So what makes that happen?

David Icke

What makes that happen is an electromagnetic field generated by the excitement of the crowd. What then starts, because about ten seconds later... a bit more maybe... I never said a word to what I was feeling to Betty Shine. She launches her head backwards and said, "My God, this is powerful. I've got to close my eyes for this one." I'm of course sitting there and I've come across none of this ever before.

She starts to tell me that she's seeing a figure in her mind, and the figure said that they knew you wanted them to contact you, but the time wasn't right. I never said a word to her that I said to them, 'Would you please contact me, because you're driving me up the wall?' She said that she was going to tell me what they were communicating to me.

It was that I was going to go out on a world stage and reveal great secrets. One line was: one man cannot change the world, but one man can communicate the message that can change the world.

There was basically a story that had to be told. That there was a mass awakening coming and this massive awakening I dubbed in my first book after this, The Truth Vibrations. Because what I was being told is that this energetic change what I now know to be an information change... a consciousness change... was going to act like a spiritual alarm clock. It was going to wake more and more people up to see the world as it is, rather than what they had been led to believe it is. And that the most awake would be touched by this first, but eventually in my words even the solid go to sleep... we're going to be affected by it.

When I look back over 25 years now, when I was in that front room with Betty Shine, there was absolutely no evidence whatsoever that anything of the kind was happening. But when I look around now, having been on the journey for this quarter of a century, I see a phenomenal awakening going on. No, it's not the majority... no, it's not even nearly the majority... but the number of people now worldwide who are willing to look at things, and look at concepts and information with an open mind rather than a concrete one.

The kind of people that are now starting to be touched by this in the sense that they're starting to think thoughts they thought they never would. That I call you people in the dark-suit professions of the system is very encouraging and certainly supports what I was told was going to happen all those years ago. And from that time in that front room, my life has been this synchronistic series of "coincidences" and walking into information in multi-various ways and multi-various kinds which has given me a picture. It's been like somebody in the unseen has been handing me pieces in a puzzle.

And it's still going on today and it's taken me into realms well, well beyond what most people perceive as normal. Most people perceive as what is real... and this lovely line that I hear all the time... beyond what people perceive to be the real world.

So the next question I say to those people is, "Okay, what is the real world?"

I think very quickly you can establish with people that it's actually the world they're being told is real. And I think it's the first step. It is a process of deprogramming, for reasons I'll come to.

The first step to being able to step out of the position of slavery is to realize that you are a slave. Because you cannot do anything about being a slave, if you think you're free... not possible.

What we're looking at is... and this goes deep in the rabbit hole, but we're looking at a mass controlled system, where the few who are controlling the many. I understand we can talk about banking scams and political scams and we can talk about that and that's fine. But they're all peripheral to the main foundation of this control system. And that is the control of human perception. To manipulate people to believe that slavery is normal, and slavery is freedom, and slavery is the real world, mate.

If you're saying that I'm a slave, you must be mad. I mean what we're looking at... I've said this in the... in the books many times... we're looking at a world that's inverted. It's an inversion. Everything is inverted, everything is upside down. So you look at the sort of things that George Orwell talked about, the concepts of control that he wrote in his book, 1984.

Basically, what are we looking at? We are looking at an inversion. When he talks about 'war is peace' and 'freedom is slavery' and all that stuff.

What we looking at, we are looking at is an inversion, its all about inversion. What I would say to people who dismiss all this and say, "Oh, it's a load of rubbish. I'm in the real world" is where does your perception of the real world come from? It starts when you leave the womb and parents most of the time... the overwhelming majority of the time. Not through malevolence, but by believing they're doing the best thing for the children. They are telling you what is real and not real, what is good and bad, what is possible and impossible.

It starts at the earliest age, the programming... the perception programming. Because what you've got there at Stage One is parents who have been through the program I'm going to describe, and accepted it as reality, accepted it as normal, then being programmers for their children out of what they think is love, not out of malevolence.

Then in a very short time, shorter all the time it seems to me, the child is into some kind of school system. Maybe three years after leaving the womb entering this reality maybe at the age of 4, they are sitting in a classroom of some kind with an authority figure telling them what's right, what's wrong, what's possible, what's impossible, what to believe, what not to believe, when you can go to the toilet, when you can't, when you must be there and when you can go home. And even pretty soon impacting upon your home life, with what they call homework.

So if you just look at it from up to this point, the child not long in this world, already the programming is very powerful. Now your schoolmates around you who are going through the same program... they will confirm to you as they accept it, that this is normal.

You'd look at how at the early stage these extraordinary, even little kids who were different in some way will be turned upon by the group often, not always, but outrageously often given how young they are when it starts. You then go through the school system which is nothing more than a reality programming system, which challenges everything that the system wants you to know, and it's not telling you everything that the system does not want you to know.

People debating all the time about how children are taught. Should it be this method or that method? But there is virtually no debate on what they are taught and what they are not taught. Why? Because the parents looking on, most of them have been through that system, so that's their norm. So the norm is okay for their children.

Then you go on to college and university and you do that at another level and all the way through you have something called exams which you are tested on how much of the programming you have downloaded. If you downloaded it really well... and what that basically means most of the time... is to pass exams... is not intelligence, it's not wisdom, it's not free thought.

It's memory, the ability to memorize and regurgitate that memory onto a paper at one specific point called an exam. Soon after that most of the kids will forget what they knew at the time of the exam. The pressure is on children more and more to pass their exams, because that's the program.

So I would say to people that say they live in the real world and anything outside of that must be crazy... I would say to them this. If you look at what human life is, against all possibility of what we really are, we are all possibility. You look at what human life is for most people. It is their own few years of relative freedom... maybe three, maybe four. But before this period, you are starting the programming the parents impose... what they believe is right... through their program onto you.

You then go to school and you are then going through the programming or the perception programming all the way through your school life. You then go into the world of so-called work. What is happening through school? We hear this more and more certainly in Britain. We hear the term: schools must prepare young people for the workplace.

What that means is not that school and education should set out to bring the unique self out of every child, so that every child can express their unique abilities, their unique gifts. No, the opposite is the case, it must model the child to fit the workplace.

So you then go out into the world of work, and you chase a career, and you're told that going up and up and up in this career, going higher and higher, getting a bigger and bigger title, and position is what life is all about. Earning more and more and more money and to achieve that, unless you've got rich parents, you have to go into terrific amounts of life-changing debt to pay for your education at university, so that you can pay for your own programming.

So you go out into the world of work and you go on and on and on. You then reach a point at which a lot of people reach later in life, where they get to these positions that they were striving through life for.

And suddenly they say, what was it all about? I don't feel any different now than I felt before. I thought this was going to give me something. I thought this is going to give me happiness. I thought this was going to give me joy, but it's not, it's just given me more stress.

So you see this program going through birth, through school, through higher education into the workplace, and on into retirement, and on into the cemetery.

Then you take another aspect of this where the idea is that you come into the world. You reach a certain age. You meet someone of the opposite sex, then you have children, then you have a family, then you go on into retirement and into the cemetery. Now I'm not saying that there's anything wrong with having those aspirations if that's what people choose to have.

My point is this, when we are in a reality... in a universe of infinite possibility... why is this considered... this program, this sequence... considered to be the only normal way of life?

You go anywhere in the world and again and again you basically come across this program. In some parts of the world, you might not come across the school university program in the same way. But you'll still come across this 'born, meet someone, get married, have children' kind of thing. So look at it, I would say to people. Look at it. It's a program.

You see, the more that I've studied this, the more absolutely convinced I am that we actually live in a computer simulation. Interestingly, there are more and more scientific mainstream, open-minded mainstream... not the centre of the mainstream, scientific studies that are coming to basically the same conclusion.

I mean, look everywhere... what we could call cycles are actually programs. Look at the cycle of any species of animal, look at what I call the natural cycles. Look at them and they are repeating programs.

The trick of the control system is to persuade you, while going from A to Z of the program, that you are doing it through free choice and free thought. What I would say to people that want to wake up from it is: "Ask yourself. Look at your life, and ask yourself how many of the decisions that directed your life and your direction were actually made through free thought? How many were made through the influence of perception, starting with the parents going through academia?"

Then of course you've got the omnipotent media that's constantly underpinning that idea. Once you start to realize... 'Actually, my free thought is illusory,' and that my faith, my decisions that I thought were mine, were actually massively influenced through my life by external factors... be it education, parents, media... whatever.

Then you come to this conclusion. I am a slave, and at that point, you can start ceasing to be one. I would say to most people, "When you wake up in the morning, do you want to go and do what you're doing today and what you have to do?"

From my experience most people are saying no, some would say yes, because they are doing what they have chosen to do. Most people will say, "Look, mate, I'm doing it because I have to earn money to live." So you do not have the choice, the free choice to wake up in the morning and say, "I'm going to do this." You have to do A, B or C, because you have to earn the money to pay the bills... not just to live, but to survive. Under any criteria... what I've just described... it is slavery.

Look at a slave that wake up in the morning and they've got to do what the slave master says. In terms of humanity, the slave master is a system which has attached humanity to it by attaching human perception to it.

Therefore there's a line in the first Matrix movie about people controlled by the matrix, controlled by the system... being so inured, being so dependent upon the system that they'll fight to protect it. That's what you see.

So, when people like me are talking in these terms, those that are the very slaves I'm talking about will dismiss it as nonsense all dangerous and seek to defend the system. It's like a slave defending the slave master. It's like a prison defending the border in the prison. But I see it all the time.

I remember once I was in a restaurant in America and I was feeling a bit playful. I was out and while I was there I wanted to point out the system for what it was about. As I looked around the room and saw no one seemed happy there at all. So what I did is I put a bread roll on my head and sat there and very quickly the waiter was over asking me if I wanted another glass of wine. And when I said yes, he said to me, "You think you might have had enough, Sir?"

So I said to him, "So I can only put a bread roll on my head if I had too much to drink, right? Well you know, I'm just taking the right to freely put a bread roll on my head. Why is that a problem?"

"No, it's not a problem."

We got into this conversation and I said to him "Think about it, do you think you're free?"

"Oh, I'm free," he said.

"Well, can you walk out of here?"

"I can't walk out of here now; I have a living to earn."

And I said, "Well, what about when you leave here, are you free?"

We went through this sequence and eventually he realized,

"Actually, I am forced to do so much that I've never thought about it before, but I am, aren't I?"

When people do that, they realize the true nature of life on Earth which for most people is a state of slavery. And that's first base. Without that, we cannot be free. Because the way the system works is that it convinces slaves they are free, and therefore, nothing is ever done about their slavery. And until it is, nothing can change.

How do you see the world today in terms of the challenges facing us?

Well, I think we're at the point where the immovable object is starting to look into the eyes of the irresistible force. The immovable object is the system which thinks it's immovable, but it isn't. It's increasingly coming face to face with the irresistible force, which is irresistible.

That's this energetic awareness... consciousness change... that is awakening people to their own slavery. My experience anyway when I was talking earlier about the people in the dark-suit professions, as I call them, are beginning to question their lives and question their perceptions and question what life's all about.

That is what I called, years ago, The Truth Vibrations. It's this re-evaluation going on in this re-evaluation, although they might not use these words. It's an evaluation that leads them to the conclusion that they are actually a slave. It's like I say the most important thing that we can first of all conclude, before we're ever going to do anything about it. So we're at the point now where this system of control, which is essentially controlled and centrally dictated, has been moving on and on and on and on through history and grasping more and more power. It's been grasping more and more power at the centre in all areas of our lives.

When you think about a few controlling the many, an absolute prerequisite to that is to centralize decision making... centralized power. Because the more points of decision making there are, the less control any few at the centre are going to have over those decisions. What we've seen throughout history and I would strongly contend that there has been a force and still is behind this throughout history... with people that have been born and died, and generations have come and generations have gone. I would contend very strongly that there is a common force and theme through all of this which is directing human society very clearly, closer and closer to total control, to do what they have to... to centralize power.

So we went from a tribal situation, and when the people in the tribe were making decisions about the tribe. Then the tribes came together, a lot of them came together into what we call nations. Now a few people at the centre of the nation are dictating to all the former tribes. Now certainly in Europe, but worldwide, too with unions and so-called trade agreements, we are bringing those nations together under centralized dictatorship. I mean the European Union is a classic example of that, where a few dark suits in Brussels are in effect dictating to the whole of Europe... dark suits in Brussels who are bureaucrats and administrators and dark suits elsewhere, in Frankfurt that run and control the European Central Bank.

So if you look at the word globalization, that is just a word to describe this process of incessant centralization of control and power that I've been talking about that has spanned the generations.

So now whether it's corporations, whether it's banks, whether its governments, militaries... increasingly with NATO and such like... the more and more we've got the centralization of control over every area of our lives. And it's becoming more and more centralised by the day through these trade agreements which are giving more power to corporations than governments, which are supposed to represent the people. So this has been going on. What's also happened is we've had more and more centralization of control in law enforcement to these various levels, be it police, or be it the military.

So this control system with the wealth and control going into fewer and fewer hands... that status quo being held together and protected by law enforcement that's ever more draconian... has been a process that is being coldly calculated, that you can follow through the generations to present day, getting more and more centralized and more and more centralized power all the time.

We have reached a point now where the irresistible force is starting to awaken people. Never before, certainly in known human history, have anywhere near enough yet, but never in known human history in my view, have as many people as there are today started to see the game. Starting to see what's happening and starting to see the techniques of manipulation and perception manipulation that manipulate humanity to accept changes that lead on this direction that I'm talking about. That's what I mean by the irresistible force of coming face to face with the immovable object, which isn't immovable, just thinks it is.

So we're at this big fork in the road where people have the choice between slavery and freedom, between going on the way that we have been, going on along this process that I'm talking about into what is planned by these very strange people... to be something that George Orwell would have said about, 'I didn't realize it would be this extreme.' Or we can awaken. Not just to the nature of what is happening and why. But most important, we can awaken to the true nature of who we are, which is consciousness.

One of the most important parts of this... what I call perception deception... is to manipulate people and program people to perceive everything only through the five senses. The five senses are the great illusion, and if people experience and perceive the world only through the five senses, the system's got them. Because in the books over the years and in the talks that I've done, I've never talked about the conspiracy to enslave humanity without talking about the nature of reality and the nature of who we are. Because unless you talk about both, there is a massive imbalance... because one is an expression of the other.

It's the ignorance of the nature of reality and the ignorance of the true nature of self that has allowed the slavery to happen. Where we are enslaved, we're enslaved in the prison of the five senses. People should look at this process I've talked about of so-called education... they should look at the media. They should even look at science... what passes for it... and ask themselves, "Why? ...when we are supposedly at the cutting edge of human awareness and capable of this so-called amazing technology."... actually it's the Stone Age really, but the so-called amazing technology. Why is it that if you stopped people almost anywhere in the world and said, "Who are you, and where do you come from?" they would probably... most of them... give you their name and tell you where they live. Others might tell you a tale related to the religion they follow.

But... and if they follow the mainstream science... they might say, "I'm just a cosmic accident after me threescore years and ten I disappear into non-existence."

What I'm saying here is why is it that the nature of reality is virtually not discussed in the schools... virtually not discussed in the media? I mean look at all the channels there are now, television channels all over the world. You go to America you can flick through for an hour and still not run out of them. You see programs and channels for virtually everything you can think of. But how rarely do you ever see any exploration of the nature of reality beyond the mainstream scientific version of reality. And yet when you take the trouble, take the choice to delve into the evidence that exists even in the most more open-minded end of mainstream science, quantum physics and suchlike, you realize that this so-called physical solid reality is an illusion.

I've been saying for years that this world that we perceive as a solid physical world actually only exists when we decode it into existence. People have looked at me, "You're mad!" Yet very recently just a few weeks ago, there was a mainstream science study which concluded... in their way of describing it... that the world that we see only exists when we look at it. When we're not looking at it, it's in a different form to that solid world that we see when we are looking at it. The word I've used over the years is not when we look at it, and decode it, it's our attention that decodes it.

> So you say to people, "OK, this is a real world, right?"
> "Yeah."
> "So, it's solid."
> "Yeah, yeah of course it is, look... solid wooden table."

Then you say, "Well, quantum physics has actually shown that it is not." Because there is no physical, it's an illusion. Not only that, the human visual perception range is so tiny, what we call visible light... it's almost laughable. So we are living apparently in a solid world that provably can't be solid. And we are seeing a sliver of frequency that we can decode into what we perceive as a physical world... it is actually holographic illusory physical. So I say then again to people, "Here you are in a world that seems solid, but it isn't." So I would say there are a few questions there for a start.

The world that you think you are seeing... the world in which you think you are... seeing everything in the space you appear to be observing... is a frequency range so tiny it's hysterical. Mainstream science says that the electromagnetic spectrum is 0,005 % of what they believe to exist in the universe in mass and energy and all that stuff. Yet some say it's a bit more but not much. The visible light which is all that we can actually perceive as this reality we see, is a fraction of the 0,005 %. So let's look at that and let's be just a little bit humble and a little bit sensible, and ask ourselves, "How can we be so sure that our perceptions that we've grown up with, of self, of life, of reality of everything, have an unshakable validity, an unquestionable validity?" ...when the world you experience as solid, isn't solid, and the amount of reality that you can actually see and perceive is so ridiculously small. For a start, if that's the real world, well, it isn't very real to me.

So again it's an extraordinary part of this perception program that, given all these things, that people can still be so certain and so immovable... that what they believe and perceive which is what they have been programmed to perceive and believe by this process of what we call life. How they can be so certain and immovable about it is ridiculous from anyone looking on. So the question is "Why does almost everyone do it?"

Well, it's because it's a program. Why does this computer in front of me now respond... when I press Enter ... in the way I know it's going to respond? If I put data into it and I press Enter, I know before I do how it's going to respond. Why, because it's programmed to do so.

When I observe the world, it doesn't matter, almost doesn't matter what culture, what race, what background. If you put the data in, you put people in a certain situation, you can pretty much press Enter and you're going to know how they're going to respond. It's wherever I look, whether it's human response, human emotional response, whether it's this process of cradle-to- grave sequence I talked about earlier. Whether it's cycles, whether it's the cycles of the animal world or the cycles of species, they're all programs. This then comes to something else when you look at the way animals live and the way humans live. They're basically the same.

Does it matter if we vote or not?

Not at the moment, no. See, this is another thing. Everything is of perception deception. So we are back here to people who are slaves, being manipulated to believe they're free so they will not rebel against their slavery. Voting and the political system is fundamentally part of this. There came a point... I mean its still goes on around the world, but certainly in Europe and the Western world... there came a point where people were no longer accepting royal dictatorships and dictatorships by individuals.

So we moved to this process of politics and what they call democracy. And the great con trick, the great 'you are free when you're actually a slave' part of politics is to equate as interchangeable terms, democracy and freedom. So democracy at its best is tyranny by the majority. And at its worst, which is much of the time, it's actually tyranny by the minority. We have a prime minister and a conservative government in Britain at the moment, that has power to win any votes in the Houses of Parliament and it secured thirty seven percent of the vote, and that's called democracy... the people deciding... or the people have clearly not decided.

When you look at democracy and political voting, just as democracy is equated with freedom, so voting is equated with freedom. But you can only do that if voting is related to choice... if you have any political party with any chance of forming a government basically standing on the same policy postage stamp as the others that have any chance of forming a government. You were not voting from a perspective of making a choice, you were voting for different masks on the same face. By voting you are giving your power and energy, and you are giving credibility to a thoroughly rigged system.

I would point people to a blatant example of this, which is George Bush, Junior and Barack Obama in the way that they were promoted, the way that the propaganda operated. You could not get two people more different than those two... especially according to the first election campaign of Barack Obama, when he promoted himself as so far different from George Bush, it was extraordinary.

But what has happened? The same policies that unfolded, that unfolded under Bush have continued under Obama. You find this all over the world. Why? Because a control system does not do choice, it does the illusion of choice, but it doesn't do real choice. So you have the illusion of choice that you go through the education system and then you decide what job you're going to do... what profession you're going to follow. You think you're choosing something. But actually all you're doing is choosing different aspects and different jobs that are of the system. Thus, you have not got choice.

What you're doing with politics is apparently having the choice of voting for different political parties, when actually you're voting for the same force... the choice is an illusion. So I've not voted for decades... since I was in the Green Party I've not voted. So I don't give it... from my personal point of view... I don't give it my energy.

I don't give it credibility by me taking it seriously. It's not to be taken seriously and people say that if you don't vote, then you don't deserve a say.

Well, actually by not voting, you're having a much bigger say than those who do. Because if people chose not to vote, the statement, if enough did it that people were not having the system as it is, would be extremely powerful. What you'd be doing by not voting is taking away the credibility of the system, instead of giving it credibility. But people think, "Well, now I get a vote, because if you don't vote, the other side will get in." Well, the other side is controlled by the same people as the ones you don't want to get in. C'mon, you know!

The biggest and most powerful statements I suggest that people can make political is not to vote on a vast scale. Because then the system has no credibility. I'm one of the reasons that around the world they are trying to bring... and in some countries they have... compulsory voting and a fine if you don't is to protect the system from just that: withdrawal of credibility. Because you hear it all the time, doesn't matter who gets it, nothing changes. Well, ask yourself, "Why is that?"

Again we are back to possibility. When you think of the possibilities of the way of running a society, the way of organizing a society, the way of organising the ability to purchase what we need. Why is it that according to politics worldwide no matter what the colour of the party... why is it that with any party... with any chance of forming a government, the same ongoing one way of doing it is always what they stand for?

They are there to give the illusion of choice to hide from people that they have no choice, that they are not free as they think... but they're actually in a form of slavery... the way the system works through compartmentalization of knowledge and to me, even to me, it's been extraordinary sometimes to realize how far up the pyramid or how deep in the rabbit hole, whichever way you want to go. You can go... in terms of people in positions of power... before you meet one that actually knows what's going on and why, because the program is

David Icke

not just for the masses. The program is for the vast majority of politicians, the vast majority of doctors, the vast majority of scientists, and the vast majority of public administrators. It's only the tiny few who actually are in awareness of the fact that there is a system with an agenda and where it wants to take us and how it takes us there. Most of them are not in awareness of that. They all will say to you, "Look, mate, I live in the real world." What it means is, I live in the program.

For me, what this world is symbolically, and actually not even symbolically... actually much of the time, is a mad house. I think what's happened is like I said in one of my books. If you're born into a madhouse and it's all you've ever known and you've never been outside the madhouse and everyone around you is in the madhouse and being brought up in the mad house... then to you, the madhouse, and all that goes on there, is normal. When someone comes in and says, "Hey this is a bloody madhouse," you think they're mad, because they are challenging your version of normal. Therefore, they must be mad.

This is why people throughout human history who have been condemned by the society of the day as mad, crazy, eccentric, have been the sane ones with hindsight. It's the same thing today. So another part of the deprogramming is not just the realisation that actually you're a slave and what you've taken to be free thought was actually not that at all, but also to realize that the world is a lunatic asylum.

What I found is... because it's an inversion, and one of its inversions is an inversion of life... the inversion of life is death, destruction... we have a world that's awash with death and destruction.

And having bombed people to death and destruction is called protecting civilians from violence. The whole world is upside down, it's an inversion. If you take balance and harmony and a celebration of life to be sanity, then what we live in is insanity.

My own experience... I found that in a very profound realization, because once you realize the world is mad, you will see and realize that it's not you that's mad. It's actually the world that you are observing. You stop trying to make sense of it. From the point of view of, "It can't be this mad, it can't be this mad, so it must be me," ... it's not. It is that mad and it's mad, because it is made to be so. Because it is systematically inverted, so you think slavery is freedom, war is peace, and all the rest of it.

What are your thoughts about money and the global banks?

Well, this is again whichever subject you bring up we come back to the same thing: illusion, deceit, inversion.

Money has been the way of hijacking our old friend... it keeps coming up... hijacking choice. If you said to most people in the world who aren't doing what they want to do, which seems to be most people, "Why aren't you doing what you want to do?" ... again and again the reply will be, "I don't have the money."

So we have the skills and gifts in people in abundance all over the world that could be used to make this world a nicer place, a better place, and a more joyous place, a more creative place, a place of limitless potential. But so much of that talent, those gifts are locked inside of people, because they cannot express them. Because what those gifts and talents are don't suit the system.

Thus the system ensures, unless you come from a rich family, that there is not the money for those things for you to actually do them. And anyway your time is overwhelmingly focused on survival. Paying the rent, paying the energy company, paying for food and surviving, and while you're doing that, you have to do what is necessary to earn that money and the system invariably tells you what that is. Your choices of what you do with your life are overwhelmingly dictated by the system, on that basis of, 'Do this or you won't have money to survive,' and so much human talent, human creativity never gets expressed because of a simple thing, money.

So this is the other thing. How many people ask themselves, "What is money?"

David Icke

When they talk about money they're obsessed with money. It's unbelievable the number of people that are obsessed with money. People with money are obsessed with money, people without money are obsessed with money, there is a great obsession with money. Everything comes down to money.

As Oscar Wilde said, "People know the price of everything and the value of nothing."

This is where the money has taken over the psyche, and it's taken over the psyche because of its importance in relation to choice and its importance in relation to survival. And yet what is it? It's simply a figment of the imagination. Money is merely a theoretical unit of exchange. So when you say to people, "How does money come into circulation?" ... then they will say something like, "Oh, it's the government, isn't it?" "Oh, I don't know... well, it's government."

I've talked to two economists sometimes and they've not been able to give me a proper answer where money comes into circulation.

It comes into circulation quite simply overwhelmingly through private banks making loans to people.

What do you think about the debt-based economy people are stuck in, and is there a way out?

Well, again, the way out starts,
A. I'm a slave.
B. I have no political choice.
C. It comes from, first of all, the understanding of most people don't have it, that money is an illusion and a form of systematic control.

Then we might have the motivation to say, "What do we do about it?"

But again until you reach these conclusions and these realisations about what it is, you don't have the motivation to put something in there that's different. I think it's very, very important that the alternative media does not believe that it's only talking to itself, because that's not its job. Its job is to talk to people and communicate information to people who have no idea of what's going on in the world. I hear people in the alternative media say, "Well, we don't need to talk about money, we know about all that."

Well, we, us, and you may do, but billions out there don't. So I make no apologies for constantly repeating these things whenever I get the opportunity. So this is what the mainstream media or the alternative media... much of which mirrors the mainstream media in the way it operates... in my view. And it's closed my ideas in so many ways, too, with honourable exceptions. It needs to appreciate that it's not just talking to its natural constituency... people who would be interested in what it's got to say. Then once it's done that, it moves on to something else.

No, it's got to appreciate that unless vast numbers of people understand the problem, they won't realize there's a need to actually deal with it. Money is another thing. I keep hearing people in the alternative media saying, "I don't want to talk about money, we know about that." Well billions don't! OK, let's never forget now. Otherwise, we're not doing what we need to do.

And with the financial system, it's like you're talking to me about the people that look close to anything alternative. Well, one of the great ways to get to those people... in my experience anyway... to get those people to look at the world differently is to start with money. Because people are obsessed with money or they have a certain perception about money. If we're going to start saying what actually the world's not quite like you thought it was, let's start with money.

What we have is a system specifically created not only to control people's choices as explained. But to hijack the world and to acquire the world by exchanging non-existent money, figures on a screen known as credit for real wealth... land, businesses, homes and all the resources... this is what has happened through the centuries systematically to present day. I would say this too, to those that say I live in the real world, this is all nonsense.

David Icke

The figures were made public recently that 48% of the world's wealth is now said to be owned by one percent of the people and it's moving on towards 50% very quickly. Because the more wealth you have, the more wealth you have to acquire more wealth.

So let me ask the people who say they live in the real world and its all nonsense, "Do you think that nearly 50% of the world's wealth being in the hands of one percent of the world's population has happened by accident? Has it happened by random chance? Or has it quite blatantly happened by certainly not random design."

So what's going on? What's going on when that can happen and that clearly has been by design. How has it been done?

By creating a banking system which is allowed to lend money it doesn't have, called fractional reserve lending where they can lend 9 to 10 times what they have on deposit in fictional money called credit and then charge interest on it... when people cannot pay back that money, plus interest... often for no fault of their own, because some economic crash or whatever. The banks can move in and take the land resources and real wealth in exchange collateral for figures on a screen, credit that never has existed and never will.

This happens on an individual level and it happens on a country level. We're looking at it now with people like Greece and other countries that are in dire economic straits and they're people going through misery and deprivation as a result of not having enough figures on a screen, worth nothing unless we believe they are worth something called credit. So this exchange of credit... theoretical money... for real wealth over time has been the way that 1% has accumulated nearly 50% of the wealth of the world. That's how it's been done.

If you have a situation where you have interest on money, you are always going to have slavery. Because this situation without producing anything in terms of production, without producing any contribution to society, you can acquire the wealth of that society by simply issuing non-existent money and charging interest on it.

That's the other point. When you go to a bank and you borrow money or credit say 50,000 dollars, that bank creates out of nothing 50,000 dollars that it doesn't have, quite legally and starts charging you interest on it. But the interest is never created, only the principal figure. So, if you think about that, every time a bank makes a loan anywhere in the world, they are lending the principal figure but not the interest you have to pay on top of the principal figure. That means something very profound, that there is never ever enough money in circulation to pay back all the principal debt and the interest on the debt outstanding. Therefore, people losing their homes, their land, their livelihoods is built into the system of finance and it's done systematically.

We need an exchange to overcome the limitations of barter which involves interest on money. I mean that's when the currency is issued as a unit of exchange, not as a debt. If you had a money system which did not involve interest on money... in which money could not be made from money... could only be made from a productive contribution to society, then a lot of these negative things to do with money in the financial system would disappear.

There have been times when local communities have been in dire economic straits have created their own theoretical currency... where someone in a recession who wants their house painted and you've got someone in a recession that has the skill to paint a house. But because of the control of money, the two can't be put together. What some societies have done in these dire straits is they have created their own theoretical money where you have a central point that's keeping a tab on it and someone goes and paints a house, that person whose done that gets credit and the person who's had the house painted goes into a deficit. So now, the person who had the house painted has to contribute to that community with their skills to remove that deficit they've got to that community. Now, the guy who's painted the house and has the credits, he can now ask other people to do things for him up to the point of that credit.

What all that is doing is creating a way of overcoming the limitations of barter. You know quite simply the guy who paints the house might not want anything that the person he's painting the house for can give to him. This overcomes that limitation and in that way it works as a means of opening up opportunity, opening up people's gifts and contributions. But once you have interest on money, once you can make money for money, once money is not simply a way of exchanging contributions to society, but a way of acquiring that society. Then you have the situation we're in now. That's how the world's been taken over, by the creation of non-existing credit and exchange for wealth that does exist.

There are ways around that. But once again people are not going to look for them, unless they realize what the situation is. Those communities that I talked about did not create those theoretical currencies operating in their community, so the system that was there before the money system collapsed, and they were in dire straits. So people have to become aware about how things are, before they have an opportunity to change it.

We have started to read and hear about microchipping people. What does that mean?

The human body is a biological computer. We perceive technology to be things with metal and nuts and bolts. But from the point of view of those behind human society, the biological is also a form of technology and these technologies can interact.

This is why you've got the whole process of what they call a computer-brain interface, where the brain can work a computer, because the brain is a very advanced form of biological computer system. Once you get technology inside the biological computer... the biological holographic computer if you like... you could externally manipulate its thought processes, its emotional processes, and its physical processes.

If you look at the body on one level, it's an electrical system, communicating electrically. Anything that can hack into that electrical system can start to dictate, manipulate, and distort the electrical communication that we call mental and emotional activity and physical activity. The idea of getting the microchip into people is to access the computer. This is what the whole transhumanist agenda is about: artificial intelligence, and it's about getting the technology of the kind that we understand as technology interfaced with biological technology, the body...so the body can be externally manipulated, and again what that means is to take the control of human perception onto a whole new level of effectiveness.

What they're looking to do with a transhumanist agenda and the microchip is an expression of that, is to turn humans into technological robots, biological robots. They have done that to a very, very large extent through the manipulation and engineering of perception in the way that we've been talking about. But the transhumanist microchip agenda is to take that to a whole new level of perception control. To the point where consciousness beyond the body is basically excluded, technologically excluded and we are seeing this preparation happening all the time.

If you look at the way technology is being created to interact with people... like Google Glass... like these Bluetooth things that people go around with in their ear, frying their brain all day... this is part of the process of preparation for the acceptance of full-blown transhumanist technological biological interface. When you look at the addiction that people have with their smart phones and tablets and all this stuff, they are the new addiction.

You can see how people are being conditioned to see this whole technological takeover of perception as a good thing, as something that equates to evolution or something equates to moving forward. When actually it's moving massively backwards into the realm of full-blown mind control with people's thoughts being entirely the result of what is being given to them, rather than what they are freethinking. It just takes everything that I've talked about so far on to a completely different level.

That's what it's about. Yet again, people don't realize that, people don't reach that realisation, this is the first base in everything. Then they'll go on buying the latest control mechanisms, called the latest Apple phone, or the latest Samsung, or whatever. Believing that it's a good thing, and believing this humanity is moving forward as a result, when actually it's moving deeper and deeper and deeper into mire of thought and emotional enslavement and entrapment.

What are your thoughts about the de-population?

Well, de-population is not theory. It's a documented fact when you see the documents of the various organizations related to what is called Agenda 21, and Agenda 2030 is updated. They are consistent in their desire to bring down the global population to a fraction of what it is now.

I mean it's well over seven billion now. They're talking anything between half a billion to a billion. When you think what that entails in terms of the population falling that dramatically, then obviously you are dealing with an extreme that beggars the imagination.

And it's not just in documents where they're calling for this so-called optimum population. The quotes of insider of various kinds, including members of the Rockefeller family have said the same that the plan is for the population to be dramatically reduced.

What we're looking at is a tapestry of things... a tapestry of events and programs and happenings which are presented in isolation as if they're all their own strand, isolated for the rest, when in fact they're all connected to this one agenda. You know people say, "Ooh, you see conspiracy everywhere." I do not. I see one conspiracy of multiple faces and multiple expressions. So we are speaking now of the Climate Change event farce in Paris in November 2015. And that is seen in isolation as dealing with human-caused climate change – which isn't happening – which should send alarm bells off to everyone.

So you've got that and you've got the belief – because of constant endless repetition in all levels of society – that global warming is caused by human activity is true. You've got the vast majorities believing that global warming is real. And when you challenge that, the question that comes back is, well they're all lying then. Well no, at core they are lying. But the vast majority of scientists and politi-

David Icke

cians and activists have believed it, because recent estimates of annual cost of the climate hoax industry is 1.5 trillion dollars. Which means that anyone who is willing to press forward with the promotion of the global warming hoax is going to be swimming in money. Not least scientists – if you're a scientist who says it's happening, then you've got a very good chance of having a very, very healthy budget. If you're a scientist saying it's not happening, then you've got a very good chance of being marginalized, having your funding cut, and being condemned, ridiculed, and silenced in various ways.

Then you've got the vast majorities who have believed in it because that's all they've ever heard. The curriculum in the education system is all confirming to people from the earliest age that it's happening. The BBC and other organizations won't touch anyone who challenges the norm and challenges the hoax even if they are a decorated scientist.

Then you've got politicians – the rank and file and even many government – some of the most uninformed people on planet Earth. And you put all that together and it is extraordinary how a blatant unsupportable lie in which they have to fix the data to get the outcome that they want. Because if they told the truth, it wouldn't stand up. It's amazing to see how a lie so blatant can be believed by so many with financial encouragement to scientists. So then the question comes, why would the authorities, the system, the hidden hand go to such trouble and spend such money on conning people into believing in human-caused global warming when it's not happening.

The answer to this is all connected into de-population and many other aspects. It's very, very important that people lose this childlike belief in the United Nations. We just had a so-called debate in the British parliament about whether the British military should bomb in Syria. And again and again you hear politicians talking about how the United Nations has said this – we must support the United Nations.

The United Nations – people need to get the background to it. The plan for the takeover of human society on a much, much greater and more profound level now involves the centralized nation of power on a global level to have world government, world central bank, world army, world currency, cashless – my goodness, is that not happening now, not least in Sweden, I understand.

So to get to that, you need to constantly centralize power and that's what we've been seeing more and more. The G20 – whatever number they come up with this year – is a defacto world government along with things like the U.N. Security Council. And we are moving along that road. Now a crucial step on that road is the United Nations. Because it's a stalking horse and a stepping stone, whatever analogy people would like to use to that world government. The more you centralize power in the United Nations and through the United Nations, the more you are moving that point forward to a fully fledged world government.

What's happened is, the world has been sold the idea that the United Nations is about bringing countries together, putting an end to war and being a force for good for peace and harmony and all those things.

As usual with life on planet Earth, the truth is the inversion of that. And what people do is they don't research, and what they do is, they get their images of things and situations from the mainstream media, from mainstream education. They don't do any research.

If they did, they would find that the United Nations is a one-hundred-percent-owned entity of the hidden hand cabal, not least families like the Rockefellers and the Rothschilds.

The first effort to introduce a stalking horse for the world government was the League of Nations. This has been acknowledged indeed by the United Nations that the Rockefeller family was fundamental to the creation of the League of Nations. When that didn't quite hold, the Rockefellers and their cabal moved on to create the United Nations. The building and the land on which the United Nations headquarters stands was given free of charge by the Rockefeller family.

The Council on Foreign Relations in America is part of a network including the Bilderberg group and the Trilateral Commission. The Council on Foreign Relations which has driven much of US foreign policy since its creation in 1921 was the creation of the Rockefeller family. But it was funded into existence by the Rockefeller family, its expenses ongoing were covered by the Rockefeller family, and the building again, the headquarters of the Council on Foreign Relations, was provided by the Rockefeller family.

Why this is related to the United Nations is that the United States delegation, at the creation of the United Sates in 1945 was described by the people involved as a roll call of the Council on Foreign Relations. Seventy-four members of the U.S. delegation that created the United Nations were members of the Council on Foreign Relations, which is a Rockefeller organization.

And wherever you look with the United Nations, you're looking at the Rockefeller family and associate families.

You don't have to know much about the world and the Rockefeller family to realize that they have absolutely no interest in peace, harmony, justice, fairness and an end to war. They just don't. So what you're looking at with the United Nations, it's not an entity that stands for what its promotional material claims it is. It is a vehicle to create and impose the agenda of these families, which is world government, world central bank, world army, etc., etc.

It's also the total subjugation of the human race in what I call the hunger games society, in which one percent or less of the population dictates to everyone else what we would call poverty and deprivation. That situation is planned to be held in place by a strata between the one percent and the population of a vicious, merciless, and psychopathic police state.

Now when you look at that structure, you can see the one percent – I mean the last figures I saw – one percent of the global population is closing in on owning fifty percent of the wealth of the world. You are seeing the austerity programs that are creating more and more of this poverty-stricken underclass pulling in more and more people who until very recently would call themselves middle class and doing quite well. And my goodness you are seeing the rapid introduction of the police state – that society I have been talking about for a long, long time that was planned to come is now unfolding before our eyes.

Now let's pull this together.

The Agenda 21 and Agenda 2030 programs are run through the United Nations. They are United Nation programs – in other words, they are Rockefeller cabal programs. In September 2015 the global meeting of countries agreed to seventeen goals in what they call Agenda 2030 – which is basically the year they want this to be in place – that if implemented would centralize power on a global level in every area of our lives.

You look at Agenda 21 which was an earlier version of it, which began 1992 in Rio de Janeiro, Brazil when this whole environmental hoax was really introduced, and Agenda 21 – again through the United Nations where its goals are implemented – would have to be a centralized tyranny to make those things happen. They would have the power to impose upon human individuality a lack of freedom and choice on a scale that only happens in fascist and communist regimes. Now here we bring it all together.

The justification of introducing Agenda 21 and Agenda 2030 which include a dramatic reduction in the population is a belief that human-caused global warming and climate change is true and is happening. Without that there can be no justification for Agenda 21 and Agenda 2030. So the reason that the claims and the data and the predictions of the global-warming cult – because that's what it is – have not happened and are not happening – is because they are not true.

They are being claimed to justify an agenda that they need a belief in global warming to introduce. So we are looking on one level at what appears to be an environmental issue. But actually that's just a cover for a political fascist, communist agenda issue. There are maps you can find on the Internet from many organizations around the subject, Agenda 21 and Agenda 2030. There is the Wildlands Project and this thing about sustainability.

What we have to do is watch the language. The language is very important. People come from this perspective with everything. They won't be wrong most of the time and that is whatever is apparently said is an inversion of what is actually happening.

So they talk about sustainability. This is the thing when you want to bring about change that if you told the truth about the change you want to bring about you know there would be a resistance against it. Then you don't present it like that, you present it in another way, you present it in the opposite way. So you talk about sustainability and who could argue with a society that is based on things that are sustainable, you don't take more than can be replaced. But that's not what it's about.

You've got on the same team those that talk about sustainability and those that want to introduce global genetically modified food, the growing of which is destroying the soil, destroying the ability of the planet to sustain life and thus, is the inversion of sustainability.

It's very important that people constantly check the inversion and see what's really being said as supposed to what appears to be said.

Because if you look at the points of Agenda 21 and Agenda 2030, they don't say we are going to centralize power in every area of your life. They don't mention what is already happening in America, in some American states like Oregon where the authority is claiming ownership of all water, including puddles after a rain storm, if they are on your land.

So when you see Agenda 2030 and you see things like sustainable use of oceans, sustainable use of water and sustainable use of this, that, or the other to bring about what they call sustainable use, it means complete control by the authorities of that resource or source or that happening.

But they don't say that. They just tell you what they want the outcome to be.

David Icke

But if you've got an ounce of brain-cell activity you just ask yourself, what would need to happen for that desired point in the list to happen? And on all of them it's global centralisation of everything.

When you look at this map of America that they want to bring about – and you can see it on the Internet – search Wildlands Project, Agenda 21 map of America, or something close to that – you see the amount of America that is designated in that map for human occupation. It's stunning in its scale in terms of how little of America – and this is a global project – would be occupied by human beings.

The great tracts of America would not be accessible by humans, but would be owned by that which controls America or anywhere else. You again can see the language in these Agenda 21 and Agenda 2030 bullet points that confirm what some of us have been pointing out for a long time that the plan is to get people off the land and into intensely occupied human settlement zones, where the accommodation would be tiny – I mean just breathtakingly small – and they are already building them.

Of course within that density you have the potential for 24/7 surveillance down into the fine detail of people's lives. When you see that map, the idea that it could happen without a dramatic reduction of the population is ridiculous.

So wherever you look, you pick up this recurring theme that the plan is for a dramatic reduction in the population.

We ignore that at our peril really, because you can look someone in the eye and face it and deal with it or you can kid yourself that it's not happening until you can't kid yourself any longer. And at that point there's nothing you can do.

This is a time for people to face the unthinkable and face what they would have thought to be insane, extreme paranoia. If only that were true. It's not. What's happening is beyond what most people can imagine.

We have reached the point now where more and more people – because of life experience and because of what is happening in the world – are starting to lessen their resistance to the fact that the unthinkable may actually be true.

What's your opinion on vaccines, and is vaccination part of the depopulation question?

Well, you see when people talk about depopulation, they can get the idea that one day billions of people are going to drop dead. Well, that's not the way it happens. It's cumulative, when you think of the minute-by-minute assault on the human body that today's society inflicts.

It's shocking that anyone is still alive. Wherever you go, there is toxicity, there is human-generated technological radiation in the atmosphere that's around us all the time and has increased by millions of times in the last few decades. You've got toxic food, you got genetically modified food which is genetically modifying humans, and genetically modified food, by its very nature, involves growing practices with insane amount of herbicides, pesticides, and toxins to allow it to grow at all.

Then you have this vaccination regime which involves a merciless attack on a still-developing immune system in the smallest of children from the earliest of ages – this tidal wave of vaccine toxicity that is imposed upon children through the first two years of life on a scale that is ever increasing and is shocking in its stupidity. More and more vaccines are being introduced for young people later on and older people later on like flu vaccines. These are poisons they are devastating the immune system in children to the point where very quickly in their lives their immune system will never be what it could be again, because it's been assaulted in a extraordinary way while it's still forming.

Now of course the immune system is what protects us and keeps us alive. Without the immune system we won't be alive. And the more that you can weaken that, the more that people are going to fall for

David Icke

things they wouldn't normally fall for, including cancer, of course. We're protected by the immune system.

But there is another point to this. Whenever you see something that the state wishes to impose without choice, you know it is part of this agenda. So what we are seeing now all around the world particularly in America and Australia is the introduction of laws that either impose by force vaccinations on children, or have penalties for not doing so.

So in America you can't go to school. In Australia they have just introduced laws that say you will not get state benefits if you don't have your children vaccinated with all the vaccines the government recommends. Well, the government doesn't recommend them except by middlemen, middlewomen in a middleman, middlewoman way. They are recommended by the pharmaceutical industry, which of course has not the best interests of humanity at heart.

So for them to wish to impose them through mandatory means puts vaccines very high on the list of must haves for this control agenda. It is without question part of the depopulation program and the mutation of the human form program. Because this is another constant – genetically modified food is mutating human DNA genetics – vaccines are, and so on, and so forth.

There is a big, big program to change the nature of the human form. It's happening cumulatively all the time and it connects into what's called transhumanism eventually.

It's vital for people to realize, if they're going to see the picture, that we are looking at a picture. We're not looking at pixels, we're looking at a picture. We appear to look at pixels, but we are looking at a picture.

So vaccines connect with GMO connect with Agenda 21 connect with Agenda 2030 connect with the global-warming hoax connect with the austerity programs connect with the accumulation of the wealth of the world in the hands of the one percent or less than one percent. These things are all connected as is the campaign of death and

David Icke

destruction in the Middle East and that's another interesting point on the same theme.

It's very well documented that the countries that have been picked off like Libya, Iraq, and Syria, etc., were listed many, many years ago before 9/11, in fact well before 9/11. Those countries have been picked off one after the other with different excuses given to attack or undermine the countries on the list.

So just as you can see if you go deep enough the reason why they're lying about global warming caused by humans. It's the same reason that Tony Blair and George Bush lied about weapons of mass destruction in Iraq. There is an agenda: the agenda is to use global warming to induce Agenda 21 and 2030. The agenda was to lie about the reasons for invasion, i.e., of Iraq, to pick off countries on the list.

This is why, wherever you look, you see lies and falsehood. They can't tell the truth, because there be a revolution in the morning. They have to lie and the reason they lie is that they are scamming the public into accepting this journey through the script, through the agenda. That's what we are seeing now, and it's all connected – all of it.

I doubt you'll be able to throw anything at me in this interview that I can't put in that tapestry. But it's all, all connected.

What are GMO's?

Well, genetically modified organisms are basically creating hybrids, or across-crop varieties, across-species fish, in everything you think.

I keep using this word inversion. Everything is an inversion, so what we're looking at is human life being inverted.

And if you go back to George Orwell's 1984 he talked about what I call the inversion. When he was talking about is the way that the authorities and state were convincing the people that war is peace and ignorance is strength and all this kind of inverted phrases. But it's not just an inversion of perception, it's also an inversion of the very basis of human life. And what you're looking at with vaccines and with genetically modified food, is an inversion of the natural order. And thus because we are – at our core – energetic constructs in terms of the body, when you introduce inverted distorted energetic information – which is what GMOs are, which is what vaccines are – you distort the energetic balance and makeup of that which is consuming them, which is absorbing them.

What I talked about in my new book, Phantom Self, I've likened it to a virus. Basically the inversion is like a virus which is like a computer virus: it's distorting everything you touch. What this is, what GMO's are, and this is why the health effects of genetically modified food in America is so overwhelming. The vast majority of food consumed in America is genetically modified. You are seeing shocking levels of health effects, because the pharmaceutical industry is connected to the biotech industry in terms of who controls it. And the medical industry, doctors, etc., are owned by the pharmaceutical industry.

You are not getting the medical profession pointing out the obvious connections between GMO and these shocking health effects.

So you can, because of that suppression, you can have big biotech like Monsanto producing these GMO's, producing these health effects. But because the medical profession is not making that connection to the public, you can have this idiot guy who is CO for Nestlé coming out and saying there is no evidence whatsoever of health effects from GMO's.

What is happening with genetically modified organisms is they are mutating in some ways slowly but surely – and in other ways quicker – the human form.

The human body is not just a body, it's not even that if you go deeper into it, but it's another thing. I've been calling the body for a long, long time a biological computer. And the computer has the ability to think for itself. This is what the human immune system is doing

David Icke

all the time. We don't sit here telling the immune system to go and sort this out all. It just does it because it has a form of consciousness, has a form of awareness, has an ability to assess information and act upon it.

The body is a biological computer and through this computer we manifest what we call thought. We manifest what we call emotion and the more you distort the balance and harmony energetically of the body – which is what all these invasions, like vaccines and GMO do – the more you are going to distort what manifests as thought perception and emotion.

If I've got a virus in my computer, it ain't going to work properly. I can type in the data I want and I can press enter. But it ain't going to do what I wanted it to do because it's distorted by a virus and this is what's happening to humans in many and various ways that I explain in detail in Phantom Self.

So, in the end, the whole conspiracy, all these strands in the tapestry are designed to control human perception. When you look at pharmaceutical drugs and of course now there is this explosion of using psyche-changing drugs for kids of the youngest ages, and for the population in general, on a colossal scale.

When you take these pharmaceutical drugs even if it's for a "physical" problem, they – so often in terms of the psychiatric ones – still have a massive effect on people's perceptions. They have an effect on their emotions, they have an effect on their thoughts ,their ability to think clearly, their ability to think straight, their ability to be emotionally stable. You take certain drugs, and you can become very depressed. You get involved with electromagnetic fields in this technological electromagnetic soup that people live in now, and it can affect your thinking.

All these sources are not just changing the human entity in the terms of what we call the physical body. They're actually changing the human entity in ways that it thinks and feels and sees and receives. And the idea is to imprison human perception and awareness in the smallest possible bubble. There are many and various elements to this, not the least of which is changing the language so we can't even articulate thoughts and express opinions in detail because the words have been taken out of circulation. It's what political correctness is all about.

When you look at the pineal gland in the center of the brain which is part of our ability to perceive and connect with reality beyond this one, one of the things that calcifies the pineal gland and stops its functioning in the way that it should in terms of expansion of awareness, is fluoride in drinking water and fluoride in tooth paste.

This is a good example of how the whole thing works. People putting fluoride into tooth paste and water actually physically doing it, won't have a clue of the real agenda. Politicians that vote for it, most of them won't have a clue. Doctors who come out and say, "Oh, it's good for your teeth," well, clearly it bloody isn't, that's for sure. Most of them will believe it. And again we're back to global warming and there's a lot of money in saying what big pharmaceutical wants you to say.

But in the shadows where it's really coming from they absolutely know what fluoride will do to the pineal gland. It will block and weaken the ability to perceive beyond this reality thus get a perspective of this reality from behind this reality. And unless we do that, then we are in this world and of it and we get all our information, we get all our perceptions within the bubble. And thus who controls the information in the bubble controls perceptions. Who controls perceptions controls the world.

So all these things are in the end focused in multiple and various ways on making human perception and awareness more and more myopic.

I've said in my books what we're looking at is a situation where in the land of the blind the one-eyed man is king. The hidden hand is the one-eyed man, because he may be clever at manipulation, but it's actually stupid, it's the village idiot, really.

So to control humanity has to make humanity blinder than it is itself. That's what we're looking at and the assault on human perception, the assault on the breadth and depth of human perception is all about making the one-eyed man the king in the land of the blind.

Do chemtrails exist, and if so, how would you describe them?

Chemtrails are another strand in the tapestry. On one level they are putting metals and potential diseases into the atmosphere which are then breathed in by the population. So here we are back to de-population. We are back to this war on the human immune system and human health. But they also contain nanotechnology and nanotechnology can be breathed in. It is well known, beyond the ability of humans to see. But these have been analysed and nanotechnology is there.

One of the expressions of nanotechnology is what we call Morgellons disease, which is where people around the world have this disease – it began in the same time period as chemtrails – where they find strands of material in the human body which are not known to the human body, where they can be pulled out, but then they just grow again. They are some kind of synthetic genetic material. It seems to me that there's a very good chance that people with Morgellons are those whose immune system is trying to reject the invasion. There is a very good chance that is what it is. Because clearly it's not only Morgellons people that are breathing in this stuff.

In my book Phantom Self I go into this area in considerable detail. This nanotechnology in chemtrails is a very fundamental part of the mutation of the human race into something very different to what it has been up to this point. The chapter I wrote on that is without doubt in my mind the most important chapter I've ever written in any book anywhere. Because if we don't get that, then we're going to be in big trouble.

Because there's something going on that is much, much deeper than even the great majority in the alternative media understand or appreciate. The time will have to come when the alternative media has to start casting aside its own bubbles and realize what is happening and the scale of it and the organisation of it. The knowledge behind it is not the work only of what we call human beings.

Please share your thoughts, David, about the environment and the current weather conditions.

There are two things you see about the environment, when people like me challenge the hoax of human-caused climate change. You get accused of not caring about the environment. I've cared about the environment my whole life. I was in the Green Party for years back in the 1980's. As I have already indicated we live in a toxic world that has been systematically made toxic because of this agenda.

I was in a supermarket two or three years ago. I went in there looking at ingredients in various things, researching for one of the books I was doing. And I found this bottle which told me that if I swallowed any of this stuff basically it's very dangerous, and I should do this, that, and the other. I was holding a bottle of washing-up liquid. So everywhere you see this toxicity.

GMO is also a form of toxicity and demands catastrophic toxicity in support of its process through herbicides and pesticides. So I am fundamentally against the toxification of the environment. I am fundamentally against pollution. But what's happened is that that pollution has been pulled in seemingly to include carbon dioxide which is a gas without which there would be no life on Earth. It's the gas of life.

You notice when they do reports on global warming, they'll show you toxicity in China and smog, smoke and all that stuff. But what's coming out of this technology and cars and all that stuff is carbon monoxide which is very, very bad. Of course what they have done is to try and sell people diesel-fuelled cars to fight global warming and of course what diesel cars do is put out particulates that are very, very dangerous to health when you breathe them in.

So if we are going to understand the global-warming scam, we need to see the difference between carbon dioxide, the vast overwhelming majority of which is natural to the environment and pollution, and carbon monoxide.

What they've done is equate pollution with carbon dioxide. Thus the gas of life becomes a gas of potential death. Did I mention inversion?

I'm very much in favor of detoxification of the environment, but with that rider about carbon dioxide.

In terms of weather conditions another thing with people who have not rescarched it and need to appreciate is how easy it is to change the weather. They've been doing this since at least the middle part of the twentieth century at least and it goes on further. Of course it's become more and more sophisticated.

There are United States military documents talking about use of the weather as a weapon of war. If you want to bring a country to its knees you can do it through extremes of weather. You can do it through engineered earthquakes. It's like being light on your feet. It's not that you see a conspiracy everywhere. But you question everything. And you ask the question: who benefits? Who benefits from this war? Who benefits from GMO? Who benefits from this weather disaster?

I put this is one of my books a few years ago. There was a film producer in New Zealand who was researching a film and he found himself in the government library. On the desk where he was he saw this document which someone had put out for filing. He started reading it and it was a document detailing experiments during World War II of exploding bombs under the sea of New Zealand to create a tsunami, a weapon of war. Now that was during World War II that he was talking about.

For instance I've never believed that the tsunami that led to Fukushima – which benefits anyone that wants to massively radiate the global environment which is what this agenda does – that that tsunami was naturally caused. I do not believe it.

This is why the more that you can focus people', the more you can do whatever the hell you like, without being questioned or challenged. Because people will not have the breadth of sense of the possible to question what you say.

They can create tsunamis?
Don't be stupid.
How do you know they can't?
Well, well...
Exactly!

So things like hurricanes and vast rains, droughts are so easy now to create. Then you have the added bonus of being able to say, "Look, it's global warming!"

There is this technology – and it's not just in Alaska now, they got versions of it around the world – it's called HAARP. Basically it heats and manipulates the ionosphere and the upper atmosphere which can do many things, including cause earthquakes.

One of the people who got the patent for this whole HAARP technology in Alaska, Bernard Eastlund, quoted Nicholas Tesla in some of these documents. Tesla was a man who we can thank for much of the current human electrical systems. He understood the nature of vibration, the nature of energy, how everything was energy in different forms. Once you realize that and these people in the shadows do, they just don't want us to believe it. That's why Tesla ended up dying penniless and alone in a New York hotel room in 1943.

You can do many things, endless things once you know that. To manipulate reality on a vibrational frequency energetic level would seem impossible to people that don't realize that that level of reality exists.

One of the things that Bernard Eastlund has said – he's dead now – about the potential of HAARP, is that it can steer the jet stream. When you look at the weather extremes that we've had in Europe, particularly in Britain in the last few years in terms of rain, the droughts in

California, and in the southern states, what the weather people have blamed them on is the strange behavior of the jet stream, that streams air currents mostly from west to east, which bring weather across America and into Europe. If you can manipulate them, then you manipulate the weather that they produce and where they produce it.

When you look at the way the jet streams have acted so strangely these recent years and the impact they have had on the weather as a result in America and Europe, then you see that the technology to "steer" the jet stream was introduced in the 1990s, just when the strange effects on the jet stream started to be documented. You put the dots together and you can see that we are now well past the point where weather and weather extremes can be blamed only on "natural" sources.

That does not mean that all weather is manipulated, of course not. But again ask the question when the weather has a massive impact in some form, who benefits from this impact?

David, do you have a practice that keeps your spirits high?

Well, it's not a practice. I don't do things like that. I have a set of reality which is my center of the wheel, which is that David Icke is an experience. What I call a human life is an experience. And I am what is having that experience. I am infinite awareness without form, without limit, without the limitations of the body or human perception. No matter what happens to me in terms of the experience, it's just an experience. It's not what I am.

If you self-identify with being human – which of course most people do – that's what they're encouraged to do – then you become the experience, and life can get very, very much more difficult. The experience becomes much more intense – and if it's a negative experience – much more destructive – if you self-identify the experience with who you are.

So I obviously – like all of us – get pulled into the human experience. But if you keep that – if you like – default position that you are infinite awareness having that experience, then you can withdraw from the experience and you can observe the experience instead of being consumed by the experience.

Because in the end you know this is just an infinitesimal fraction of infinite reality. If you can see it in those terms, then the power comes to you. Or you can get pulled into the fact that "I am human" or "I am a man, I'm a woman" – the labels just keeps getting smaller and smaller in which case you will not live life, life will live you. In other words the program will live you. That for me is my default position which keeps me going when life can get stressful.

David, seeing the madness around me I feel hopeless. Can you suggest some ways that would help me regain my trust in the future and how to act to make a positive change?

I think trust in the future is trust in something that doesn't exist. There is no past – there is no future – that's just part of the program – part of the perception program. There is only the now moment. When you think of the past, you're in the now. Worrying about the future, you're in the now. When what you call the future comes, you are still in the same now that you were in when you were looking into the past and the future before. The scale of illusion of this reality is absolutely staggering, and actually I find it funny – the level of illusion.

Life is much easier than people think. They have been told it's difficult because if you have a perception that life is difficult, then it will be difficult.

My life experience has shown me that if it's difficult, forget it. If it flows and it's easy, then go with it. And it's crucial to doing anything. The energy of intent is a very, very powerful energy. If you have the intent that you want to do something, you want to make a difference. You want to make your contribution to whatever you choose. Then that intent, if it's genuine, not just nonsense and words, will draw to you what you need to achieve that intent. You will draw to you the people, the knowledge, and the opportunities.

David Icke

What kind of spooks most people though is even if they get that far, what life brings towards them can sometimes be what they would rather not experience. So they drop that idea and go back and say, "Well, it's nothing I can do." No, no it's not nothing you can't do, it is nothing you have chosen to do. Because one of the things – the key things, the foundation thing – to making a difference in the world is making a difference in yourself. The more that people can disconnect themselves from the program, the greater contribution and benefit they can be to others in the program.

For instance, my life has not been just me researching things and writing books. That's an outcome. Alongside that it has been a endless stream of often challenging personal experiences which have helped to peel the onion rings of programming and false perception, and have allowed me more and more as the process continues to see the world more clearly and clearly for what it is. So the researcher and the life journey of the researcher are fundamentally connected.

I see many people in the alternative media who want to do the research, but don't want to go on the journey. That means that eventually they reach a point where they can go no further, because they can understand no further, because the programs they have chosen not to deal with are blocking that further expansion into greater awareness.

So what I would say to people is this. I remember at the start of my journey, when I was blinking into the headlights of this, the psychic who was doing a reading for me said this – this is 1990 now right at the start – she was being told to tell me the spiritual road is tough, the spiritual way is tough, and no one makes it easy.

People can get confused by "Well, I'm spiritual, I want to be spiritual so I should be walking down the lanes with birds dropping on my shoulder and beautiful butterflies around my head."

What happens is all hell breaks loose. What happens is life says, "Okay, this is what you want ,this is what you need to achieve what you want" – and invariably, it's a massive deprogramming operation, which can be very challenging and very difficult.

David Icke

But if you don't go through that – some people call it the "dark night of the soul" and all that kind of stuff – then you're not going to have the capacity to understand the world, because you're still going to be in the world you're trying to understand.

You can't understand this world from only being within it. You have to expand your awareness to the point where you're looking into this world as well as being in this world, because that's the only way you can see it. You can't see a picture by putting your nose on the canvas. You can only see the picture by taking steps back and seeing the whole thing. You can't do that while you're in the program, because the program is there to stop you doing that, that's the reason for it.

So the sequence for me is to decide what people want to do, have the intent to achieve it, and then strap in and go where it takes you. Along with the challenges you deprogram will come the opportunities to do what you want to do. It's not that you have to completely deprogram and then there are no more doubts, but you have to deprogram and then you start doing things that are simultaneous. It's just that what you do becomes more and more powerful, the more you deprogram.

If you could plant one seed in the mainstream mind, what would that be?

"You've been had."

David Icke

What you allow is what will continue. Face your fears and do it anyway.

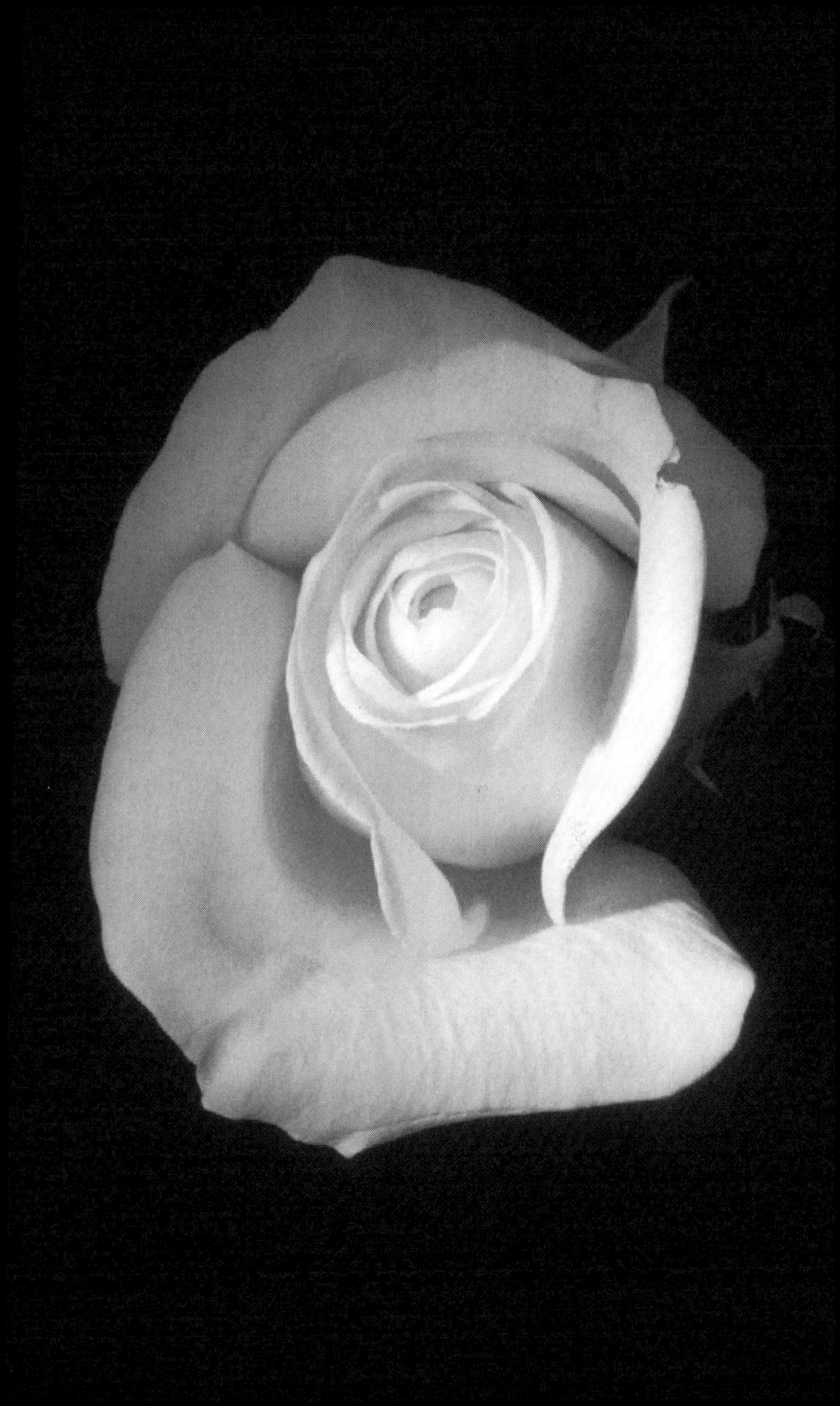

KERRY CASSIDY

KERRY CASSIDY

Introduction

Kerry Cassidy is a documentary filmmaker/investigative journalist and well known radio talk show host of Project Camelot Whistleblower Radio. Her website is very well known in the alternative media sector.

She speaks at conferences around the world and has produced several highly regarded Camelot conferences with the trademark name *"Awake and Aware"* featuring key witnesses and researchers that are part of the Camelot history of interviews.

Kerry travels the world conducting interviews and documenting the testimony of whistleblowers with above top secret clearances as well as authors, researchers and experiencers covering conspiracies, the secret space program, black projects, ETs, kundalini and ascension and free energy.

www.projectcamelotportal.com

When did you start exploring your field, was there a specific event that led you to this path of waking up?

This is a rather difficult question, because basically, when I came on to the planet I was already unusual in the sense as far as I can tell that I questioned everything. And I was very much aware of an alternative Universe. That what we could see in front of us was only part of reality and that there were unseen worlds. I was very much an intuitive child and in touch with unseen worlds. So they factored into my everyday life.

Even growing up I knew more than I was supposed to know. And I started looking even into books that my parents had sitting around that weren't kid's books, getting into the occult. I was quite young around I think ten or eleven. Somehow I had an intuitive knowledge or and understanding of what I was seeing.

So I also believe I was being abducted at a young age. I was having what I now see and recognize as some typical abduction scenarios. So I had a recurring nightmare in which I was going down a little path outside my house. There was a gate, I would get to the gate. There was a man in a top hat and overcoat standing on the other side of the gate. And I would hear a loud buzzing noise. Basically I would be terrified, – absolutely terrified – and at some point would wake up from the dream. I had this recurring dream up until the age of twelve or maybe a little longer and then one day I kind of went through the gate consciously and went beyond it, and at that point I stopped having that nightmare.

I have a strange birthmark on my arm that most people haven't seen. It's a very obvious birthmark – it's quite elaborate. It's actually called that – what's called a human Shemma. It was looked at by doctors at Stanford, because I grew up in the Bay Area, I was born in Palo Alto. California. It's a network of capillaries close to the surface of the skin that are bluish color.

At any rate I had an implant in that arm that showed up when I was young, and I had some incident in which there were some kids playing out in my yard. They were playing with a B.B. Gun, and I got in my head that I was shot by the B.B. gun when I really wasn't. But somehow, there was lost time and I don't understand what happened. My shoulder was very painful and I had this round implant thing that ended up inside my arm. And eventually it kind of travelled down my arm to the lower part of my arm, or that least that's what I thought happened.

So there were these kinds of anomalous occurrences, and I was just very aware that there was other things going on, because I think that abductions probably contributed to that understanding.

So already I was in that headspace, and I was not one of those kids who then forgot about it and started acting normal. I actually incorporated that into my worldview, and so I constantly perceive the world simultaneously through being in everyday reality and at the same time perceiving these other dimensions of reality where I was conscious.

I even have things where, not that long ago, I'll wake up in the middle of the night, and I'll be yelling "Get out, get out." And I'm talking to ETs and ghosts that are just crowding around the room or whatever. I was something of an empath growing up. I pretty much controlled a lot of those kinds of symptoms, if you will.

And my mother used to call me – this is so stupid – but she used to call me, Know-it-all Kerry, because I acted like I knew everything. I don't feel that way anymore. When I was a kid, I really did act like that, and I really did think like that – I don't know why – a little like the girl in Harry Potter, I always thought.

So anyway that's kind of a long answer to your question. Then what happened was I worked in Hollywood for nineteen years. Eventually reached a glass ceiling where I really couldn't go anywhere and I had worked in all aspects of production. I ended up doing development for a low budget film company. Then I started going off on my own and I started shopping projects around Hollywood. And they were all based on a sci-fi kind of model. This was before I got into Project Camelot, so I was shopping these projects as an independent producer to places like Steven Spielberg's company, Kathleen Kennedy, who's head of his development at that time. And with let's see, Ridley Scott – he is head of development, and James Cameron's had a development.

I had projects like WingMakers, which is the Ancient Arrow Project – wingmakers.com, it's called – it's a cool website about a black project scientist that goes on the run.

So I was doing this before Camelot. I also got a hold of somebody who became one of my interviewees, when I got into Camelot, called Dan Sherman. I got in touch with him. I found his book on the Internet and I read it. It was an e-book and I got hold of him and his screenwriter, and we took a project and tried to get that made, based on his book.

Then later, I interviewed him as part of Project Camelot. He's quite well known at this point, I believe. Again I know I'm answering this in the long way. But trying to explain that I was going down this road, I also got very heavily into researching the occult when I was in my teens.

I was also researching spiritual things, such as the Eastern philosophy, that would be a good catchall for the kind of investigations I was doing. I read things like the Mahabharata, the Bhagavad Gita, and investigated the I Ching, the Tarot, the Crowley stuff specifically, which is highly occult and so on.

So I was quite into all of that and I learned a great deal. That served me very well when I got into Camelot, because there is a backbone to everything that goes on in this sector that has to do with the occult – that a lot of even UFO researchers never had researched before they got into the UFO field, and found themselves kind of like a fish out of water in a certain way.

Whereas I had that background, so I understood about the Illuminati instantly, I knew how they think, what their philosophy is based on, and so forth. So I was a little unusual in that way.

After Hollywood, just by some weird serendipity, one might call it fate, I was given a job working as a communications manager as a contractor for JPL, Jet Propulsion Lab, which is obviously part of NASA and Cal Tech. I did a number of things over there. I worked there on and off for years, eventually even working as an executive assistant for various scientists in the lab, as they called it.

At one point I know I was tapped by a secret division that was looking into possibly hiring me, and I think I successfully blew that.

But at any rate I did a great deal of research, and I wrote screenplays while I was working on some of those jobs, because I had a lot of free time.

I know this is a long explanation, so all of that worked into Camelot. Ultimately as I say I was doing this as an independent producer. I was working to try to get movies off the ground, because I believe that making movies was the best way to clue people in as to what is really going on the planet. So that was ultimately my goal and I was having a very hard time getting there. As a result I became a very frustrated filmmaker. I actually went to film school, and it's the UCLA executive short film fiction film program. I was selected competitively to go to that program and graduated from it and also did the executive program and M.B.A. program at UCLA. And that was another thing that I did to back everything up with the business background.

At that point I decided to pick up a consumer-grade camcorder, because my mother passed away, and I had a very small inheritance. I was very frustrated as a filmmaker that I couldn't get anywhere in Hollywood shopping my projects, which I knew were very good projects. And I decided to go to UFO conferences as a lark to start interviewing the speakers and see if they had actually seen a UFO. Because I noticed that when I started going to these things that they would talk a long time about their investigations of this, that, and the other thing, but they would never talk about having actually had their own experience of seeing a UFO. That was an entree into interviewing people like Rich Dolan and Jim Marrs and so on, and I found I was good at it. This is the bottom line.

So one of the interviews I did at that time was with Bill Ryan, who became my partner in Project Camelot. I came to him during a conference. I set it up with him ahead of time. He had just been interviewed by a whole film crew with all the lights and the bells and whistles and cameras and the whole set up. And I just came up to him with a consumer-grade camcorder in my hand – just me – and said I was ready for the scheduled interview and of course he was somewhat surprised that that was going to be the set up, but that was it. So I filmed him in my hotel room and we ended up hitting it off. We went to dinner afterwards and became friends. And that interview was very well received on the Internet. He liked it very much and so did a lot of people.

So that was basically one of my first Camelot interviews. I did a couple other interviews also, one with Bill Hamilton that's still on the Project Camelot website. And one with Robert Stovall that I released years later that is on Camelot was well. These are well known names in the UFO fields.

So that was kind of my introductory. But basically to say that there was no one day or one incident that made me fall into this area. I kind of was working my way into this area my whole life.

Had I had the success I wanted to have in Hollywood, I still would have made sci fi blockbusters, and I probably would have made darn good ones. But I have to say that I would not have gone down the rabbit hole the way I have. I was forced to find another way. And in the process stumbled on what was a great idea that Bill Ryan and myself had together really at the same time in the site of the former home of King Arthur – one of them, Tintagel, England – where we basically agreed to put our skillsets together.

And to try to change the world, and the way we decided to do that was by releasing whistleblowers' – if we could find them – testimony about what was really going on, and we were already both schooled about the ET reality, about you name it.

People always ask me if I've come across things that have blown my mind or all this kind of things. And the answer is no, and I'm always sad to say that, because I know people are dying to hear that you are just blown away, you couldn't believe it. But because I had researched everything for so long, and because I had that childhood that was involved with this thing, I think I had like a natural deeper knowledge of what I was headed for, and what the world was all about, so that guided me.

How do you see the world today in terms of the challenges facing us?

I think the greatest challenge is getting the truth out to the masses. And also their willingness to want to hear the truth.

So that's kind of the backbone on which everything sits on the planet at this time in my opinion. I always believed you know, I don't know if it was really Jesus who said it or one of the Jesus's, because there's more than one that supposedly were incarnated to fill that role – a sixth dimensional Jesus and a ninth dimensional Jesus. But the truth will set you free.

Humanity has been enslaved, I think, for a good part of the time that it's been on this planet. I do believe there are many seedings of humanity to the planet. That our trajectory on this planet goes back thousands if not millions of years, probably millions of years, if I understand it correctly.

What I can say is that I do base that on some very important books that I always recommend when I do speaking engagements, which are the Voyager books by Ashayana Deane. I think that is surpasses the Bible as a much better history of much truer history of humanity that ever been written. That information was communicated to her by a race of Guardians – they call themselves – for Humanity, and they are groups of races – not one race. They are keeping our highest interests in mind, so to speak, as we progress here on this planet.

And in innocence they are our progenitors, they are our DNA. Humanity is a grand experiment and I believe that we are ET's.

Kerry, does it matter we vote or not?

Well I mean if the way I would answer that is just to say that I use a different technique to determine the answer to any question. First of all, if you understand that time is simultaneous and physicists will tell you this. And that we are seeing this, like this moment from moment to moment, we are seeing in a linear way, we are living these moments. But we all come from Source and return to Source. So if you acknowledge that as a premise then you understand that with time being simultaneous then we are all Source and we have access to all knowledge.

Therefore, if we listen to our inner knowledge and our higher self, as some people will call it, then we can access answers to any of the questions we have. At any given time the answers may be different depending on this human.

My understanding is we have at least twelve simultaneous incarnations of ourselves at any given time on this planet, going throughout time, if you see time as a huge spectrum. Then you can say that you can access each cell as we think of it, like I am myself here now. This Self is going through, in a sense, a learning curve or participating in a learning curve for self awareness and self realisation and enlightenment.

Therefore if I want to know if I should vote I'm talking about this Self in here-and-now reality. Then the answer might not be quite so esoteric as I've already kind of outlined. It may be more specific. So you may say, "Well, this self at this time will find meaning in voting as being some gesture that could turn the tide in some selection process." But that would be only if it's not interfered with by what is a kind of a global mafia or cabal, that is running the planet with a number of negative ET's behind them. Now there are positives ET's in that spectrum as well. But they operate differently than the negative ones do.

So if you're going to vote, then you have to keep in mind that at this time we're not looking at a new world government or a new world order in the future – we're there – there is a new world order. They do run the planet. And if anything they are at times losing grip on that, on running the planet right now. In fact we're in the process. In fact we have become what is known as an ascension planet since 2012 and even as we speak. So that means that they're not fully in control of humanity anymore. But they are fully in control in various aspects of our lives and, for example, if you're talking about the United States, our president is elected – he's put into office by the Cabal at this time.

So I don't believe voting makes a damn bit of difference, one way or the other, in this country.

In other countries you have dictatorships which are at least as bad as the U.S., if not worse. And in some countries, you have something that looks like a democracy, but isn't maybe in all countries.

So the question, "Should we vote?" I know I've given a very long complex answer to that. But that's really how I think about it, with all these parameters.

What are your thoughts about money and the global banks?

Well, money is energy, and there's a lot of manipulation happening. Energy is key here on the planet, because energy is the "tulip" of those with power who want to exercise power. They do it through the use of energy. So whether it's money or it's accessing the vortex or using your chi as an individual or through magic and kundalini activation etc., all of this is energy and use of energy. And then of course, we have nuclear energy versus free energy etc. etc.

So about the global banks and the monetary system, I can say it's such a complex problem, because you have gold on the one hand which is more than just a metal. It is something that empowers space travel, and because we know we have a secret space program. Various countries have their own little secret space programs, but, there is one major one, which is run by the US, Russia, Britain, Germany, France and a few others working together. That's the main earthly secret space program.

The Chinese obviously have their own. India is trying to develop one of their own. So all that relates to when you're talking about the global banks and the money and gold. Gold has been used through the centuries by the Anunnaki – monoatomic gold – to increase longevity easily. And supposedly to be put also in the skies to ward off radiation from the sun. There are traces of gold in our chemtrails now in some places.

So what I would say about that is there are huge stashes of gold and lots more gold on the planet than they give credit for in the mainstream. So in the mainstream world they will say gold is limited. The Anunnaki are still interacting with our planet. From what I understand gold is still being flown off bases and runways in South Africa, for example – I have whistleblower testimony to that fact – being flown off the planet. Gold is as I say used heavily in space travel, so it's an element or a metal that's being traded with even off-planet races, I would imagine on a regular basis.

But in general this whole game is not just dependent on what appears to be the bankers that are running the scene. What I understand is that the Rothschilds own almost all the banks in the world, so behind the scenes they're running them. There are lower level managers that may appear to be world players.

The Rothschilds are also in a sense – if you look at the pyramid of control – still a step or two down from the top level as well. So I do know that China's move is to take over the reserve currency and to try to be in charge and that there is an ET group that is trying to facilitate China running the world at this time.

I have just recently done an interview with Kameran Fally, who's part of a Kurdish family who were based in Iraq and had dealings with all the different regimes in Iraq including Saddam – who they didn't get along with – Saddam Hussein. But they have been heavily involved in the Illuminati, Bank of England, City of London, dealings with the Illuminati in the banking trade. And the interview with him recently says that there is now a blowback on the Chinese who are trying to take over the banking system.

And that this recent effort that the Chinese are all part of is going to fail, because the Cabal is now hitting back. What happens with the fallout of all of that will be this year. Actually we're going into 2016 now, according to Kameran. But that's their perspective on themselves right, so that's what they believe.

Whether there will be another element thrown into that mix that then throws both of those factions off – if you will say – I don't know, but it's highly likely, because there is a positive side that's operating all the time to orchestrate things and make sure that humanity still progresses, that humanity is not held back, and that the change will be somewhat balanced. They don't interfere in a very unequivocal way. They are not unilateral in the way they act. They influence individuals to then help them make certain decisions that would be positive and allow things to happen that way.

The negative side is working through individuals as well. But the negative side is more willing to act unilaterally to take a strong karmic step, so to speak, where they will take an action that will then influence things directly. Whereas if they are truly a positive ET or positive entities of any kind, that's not how it operates. It operates more through influence and through a mutual agreement with the humans, so to speak. So it's different, but at any rate, that's my answer to the monetary system.

What's going to happen in a year's time, I don't see the US being bankrupt as it's purported to be. I interviewed not that long ago Catherine Austin Fitts, and I was very happy when she revealed that she has quite a bit of knowledge about the secret space program, and does understand that there is a huge monetary side to that program, some of which is based on things like hidden stashes of gold, off-planet travel, off-planet land excavation of minerals on various planets. And also to say nothing of what they're doing with high yield investments that they are basically running and getting a lot of money from.

It's a huge game and I don't think it's so cut and dried. I don't think like tomorrow I'm going to wake up and everything is going to be down to zero, so to speak, in the United States, although they very likely will hit the American dollar at some point. The strange thing is that they have been planning to do this or somebody's been threatening to do this for ages now, and the opposite has been going on.

So because we have these factions fighting back and forth with each other... how this all plays out is just not clear.

What do you think about the debt-based economy people are stuck in, and is there a way out?

Well, I would say the bottom line is creativity, your own creativity. That I think we're very quickly moving into where we will no longer work for the man, so to speak. That humanity will have to create its own way of making it in the world by employing themselves doing something that they think is valuable and giving to humanity, and through that getting the means by which to live. That's how I live. And I decided to do that, I took a leap of faith when I got into Project Camelot and so did my former partner, Bill Ryan, who was in Project Camelot with me for the first three years pretty much and then the last fourth year of working with him, we basically fell apart and had different philosophies and grew apart.

So now, I've been operating Camelot for ten years and doing it on my own with the help of a webmaster. Sometimes it's someone helping with editing or depending on what the circumstances are. When I travel now, I have a partner, a boyfriend who is doubling. He's a musician, but he's doubling as a camera man and editor, a co-editor of my interviews and so on.

So debt-based economy, look, the world can change, the regimes will change, but, it's going to be up to us to create our own reality and to make a living. Living and serving humanity. So I think that that's going to be the only solution. There's no doubt whatsoever that even under this current economic model that humans are fast becoming less crucial.

And once we have these 3D printers that are en masse. They're now in small numbers in secret space programs and various other places where they can manufacture a house or whatever it is you need. Eventually there's no doubt whatsoever we will be able to materialize anything that we need.

And free energy is just the tip of that iceberg, so to speak. There's some thought that free energy is not really free, that there is a payback or some kind of cycle in which you use the energy and that goes back and has to be recycled and so on, that there are various different modes of so-called free energy. So it depends which one we end up using here en masse on Planet Earth. But there's no doubt that without all of that already having been discovered and so on – I mean it was around since the time of Tesla of course and before that – forever really – was rediscovered, I guess you might say, by Tesla.

I mean what humanity is doing is remembering. We all have the knowledge. We're in the process of remembering the knowledge and much the knowledge was lost or hidden over the last few hundred, even thousands of years. And now it's being rediscovered, and it's being brought back to humanity through our ET interactions – reverse engineering, obviously with their craft and every other technology that we've basically paid for, in some cases, with human lives – through deals with the ET's, who have abducted our children, used them for food and breeding purposes in trade for technology – that's the dark bargain that the military have made.

We have started to hear and read about microchipping people. What does that mean?

Well, I have whistleblower testimony about this. So what I can tell you is that microchipping is probably – even at this time – outmoded technology, because we each have a signature, an energy signature, that can be read by an artificial intelligence that the surveillance technology is far beyond what has been revealed by Edward Snowden in the mainstream. He's only revealing the tip of the iceberg. There is a quantum level of the surveillance technology that involves artificial intelligence and therefore chipping us with some kind of clear chip is really for the lower levels of law enforcement and things like I guess monitoring you at an airport or something where you have a chip. You have a chip right now on your passport and in your credit card. So they don't really have to chip you, per se.

So I think that eventually that's going to go by the wayside – that notion. But it's been a big scare to a lot of people for a long time. And of course they do track animals right now by putting chips in them, as you may know – pets.

I do see them advertise it – to do something with their children – to track that they'll help you find your child. These are again lower levels of surveillance technology. That's what we're really talking about. The higher levels have less need of this kind of thing.

So what are your thoughts about depopulation?

I think that depopulation is a mind-control meme, if you will, that has been perpetrated through actually even the employees of the secret space program have been fully programmed with this notion. I have witnesses that will rant on to me about depopulation, and how important it is, because we're over populating this planet. I think that's a complete illusion.

I think that scarcity is the model that our worlds have been based on, based on an Illuminati premise that goes back thousands of years. And that again – that's an illusion, as well.

The Earth is a living being and replenishes herself and we energetically are hugely powerful energetic beings that bring energy to the Earth. If we serve her well and properly, then she will also be enlivened by our presence – and plants and animals, the same thing. We know that oil, for example, is a natural resource that replenishes itself.

Again scarcity is a fear-based model that is reptilian in nature and was an illusion sold to humanity so that we would think – just like death is an illusion – so that we would believe in a certain form of reality that made it more possible for them to control us as a whole. So I think the same thing about of scarcity and depopulation – they go down the same rabbit hole.

What's your opinion on vaccines, and is vaccination part of the depopulation question?

Vaccines have been used to – yes – contaminate various races in particular with various diseases and to lower the immune system's response, so that chemtrails could have more of an effect and eventually to basically implant nano in humans. That's one of the things going on with the chemtrails. So vaccines serve that purpose, too – again, to weaken the immune system – but also to cause diseases and do away with certain portions of the population.

The AIDS epidemic is a disease which is a depopulation disease that they try to put into depopulation, but it didn't work. They've had several false starts and these plays with various diseases.

So vaccines are absolutely a way of poisoning. Also in changing this – I guess you might say – the DNA signature – turning off certain portions of DNA for children that would become active later in life or as they grew up. I think that vaccines are very diabolical.

What are GMO's?

Well, basically they are hybridization of plants by certain techniques to make them more fertile and grow larger. It seems that to be large is always the goal of GMO's. But I'm not a scientist, so I don't know the technicality of what the GMO's are supposed to be. I know that it's going into our seeds that are growing plants even. It's basically false food – I mean at the root.

So you're talking about humans trying to change the human DNA signature and consistency so that we do not get the health benefits from eating food that we would normally. It poisons our food chain and again depletes our ability to withstand any kind of control mechanisms, making us weaker.

I mean certainly they send huge populations of young men off to war to get rid of them, because they could be a serious adversary. And we're talking "might against might" here – if they were to stay at home and become discontent – so war is one of those filtering mechanisms in which they get rid of large numbers of able-bodied young men.

I just had a whistle blower contact me and say the draft for women in the US is going to go through this year or something like that. And consequently the US is gearing up for a major war with China and possibly Russia, although I question that portion, because of some of the Henoch prophecies that happen to be fairly accurate up to now – that was the Pleiadians that contacted Billy Meier – who revealed a number of things about our future.

Trajectory if we should continue on a certain path and one of those prophecies was about a coming war with China and Russia, but that Russia would change sides, so that initially Russia would be on the side of China, and eventually they would change sides. So to get back to the point, I can say that we're looking at that in the future.

Do chemtrails exist, and if so, how would you describe them?

Certainly they exist and they have been inundating our skies for at least the last ten, probably fifteen years at least. They are part of a weather wars weapon as well, so that's kind of a weapon in the arsenal of governments and high level governments even to – kind of – direct things their way. Chemtrails are also used to track incoming and outgoing craft, because the military has a great desire to be able to control our skies, even though they are fairly powerless to do so.

So the chemtrails have increased their ability to survey the skies and they purposely cause – for example, they'll cause a great deal of cloud cover on a certain area after chemtrailing it in order to hide – what I say are – the battle with the various ET's going on above our heads in daytime and at night.

So chemtrails serve that purpose as well as, of course, what I said before, which is weakening the immune system of humanity and possibly some other purposes, that do have to do to some degree with incoming planetoids and even asteroids. I think that they can use chemtrails for many purposes now.

Recently in my interview with Kameran Fally he is actually being very much read in with regard to the Illuminati. He has been contacted by at least his Illuminati contacts that told him that chemtrails were going to cease in the near future. And sure enough the reports are that there are fewer chemtrails now than there were, say, six months ago. And that the Illuminati has withdrawn funding from a certain amount of that.

But why, you have to ask yourself, why would they do that? Because they don't do anything that doesn't serve their purposes. So there may be many sides to that answer, and on one hand, it could be that they discovered a more invisible way of creating what is a chemtrail and affecting the weather. That's one thing. Another thing they're saying is that they may have achieved their objectives, which is to create a humanity 3.0, which is a humanity that is like a super soldier on the one hand, but highly controllable on the other and almost passive in nature, except when triggered.

So it's an interesting type of human that they're looking to create. They certainly want to do away with a large number of the older populations – people over the age of fifty in many cases – although they are keeping a memory in a intellectual bank, because they realized at a certain point that eliminating all the older people wouldn't really serve them, because there are a number of really good brains in the older population. And that they don't think the same as the younger population, but their way of thinking may still be highly valuable – as valuable as the new modes of thinking that some of the younger star seeds are coming in with.

So there was a change in midstream there, but generally speaking, they do want to eliminate a large portion of the population that are older eventually.

They have to fight with Big Pharma over that, because Big Pharma does not want any diseases to be cured. They don't want cancer cured, and they don't want – you name it – cured; they want all the old population to die slowly. So they'd like them incapacitated early on from fifty onwards, so that they can pay a lot of medical bills, so that Big Pharma can make a lot of money, and a lot of that money can go into what is black projects. Research into nano- and bio-computers and – you name it. So that's really is just like a money cash cow kind of thing.

Please share your thoughts about the environment and the current weather conditions.

Well, ninety percent of our weather at least for the last fifteen years has been orchestrated and manipulated by governments. And by higher level secret space programs etc. And in the same country, you will have a government operating what I call the surface government. Then behind that you will have a secret space program government which is basically the Illuminati.

The regular government is also infiltrated, but it is actually run by a higher level, which is the secret government. So when you look at things that way, you're looking at a different way of orchestrating weather, of orchestrating banking – you name it. It's all being orchestrated and manipulated.

I had one whistleblower who said the North American continent is run by one man. Russia and the Eastern Block is run by another man, and Africa is run by another.

In other words the huge areas of our globe are being orchestrated at the very top levels by one person, who is then run by – God knows which – ET's and so on.

But there are ET groups that are at war with each other in this mix as well. So you can't just stop there and go, "Well they're run by one ET group, or two ET groups." Certainly the reptilians – what are known as the Reptoids, which are humanoid looking Reptilians – are heavily involved to some degree.

We know that the mantids – the praying mantis beings – are involved and the ant beings are involved. The Pleiadians have fallen back, from what I understand, and for quite a while now, and stuck back, but they're still involved. But again they're more positively based to some degree, although there are elements.

I mean this thing is a huge mix, I guess you could say, if you painted with a wide brush. There's the Luciferian contingent that is a group of various races that do not have humanity's best interests in mind. Then there are the guardian races that do. So there is a war of worlds going on.

Do you have a practice that keeps your spirit high?

I guess you could call it that. I know it sounds crazy, but I am an extremely optimistic person. And in my own everyday life, I'm actually very upbeat. See, I get energized by the challenges here. I know that some people find that hard to believe. And I don't even know why I do it, it's the way I'm made, you might say.

In fact, I am, I guess, if you want to have a type, I am a contrarian. If you tell me its black. I'm probably going to look and see if I can find out how it might be white, red, or yellow, and I don't obey. I don't follow orders well. I never have, ever since I was a child. To me, if you tell me I can't do something, I'm going to try to find a way that I can, on purpose, just to prove that it can be done.

So because I have that nature. it does mean that if you give me something adversarial, it doesn't mean I don't get depressed or upset over something if something horrible happens. But also I almost always can see the other side of it, for one thing. I see that despite negative happenings, the light always prevails.

That just proves itself again and again.

And because I am psychic. Through kundalini, when I was twenty one, I decided I wanted to reach enlightenment. I didn't have any teachers or anything I just somehow knew I needed to do this. So I sat, basically I was living in New York City. I had access to a place to live where I didn't have to pay rent. And I was studying acting at night and I was working during the day when I could. They were temp jobs in the movie business for a while, and eventually, I just stopped working for like around a month, maybe a little less, and just meditated day and night, and I eventually connected all my chakras and I had major Samadhi experiences and Nirvana.

And I had a lot of world-changing experiences, so I see the world differently. Even though I also saw differently when I was child, after that experience, it was set in stone. I basically reached a certain level of enlightenment, I think you could say. But to me enlightenment is not a destination, it's a journey. So it's ongoing and certainly going from a human and individual enlightenment to a godlike enlightenment of source.

There are miles to go before you sleep. So I would say it's a journey. But it gave me insight, a permanent insight, into what's really going on here.

And this game on Planet Earth is all about an enlightenment. There is nothing else. You know at the absolute bottom, when all is said and done that's all that it's really about, which is the journey back to Source.

So if you want to call it a practice, you could, but it's really part of my makeup. It's the way I view the world. I don't have to practice it, I am it, it's me, it can't be divorced.

So yes, I still meditate, if you want to know some things I do that I think are positive for myself. I have a regime that requires that I play. I think play is at the root of what humans should be doing all the time, and play is synonymous with creativity. So if you're not playing and getting joy out of whatever you're doing, you're not living fully and probably not even living correctly.

But some people get a lot of joy out of suffering. So I'm not going to take that away from them, either. I do have a Zen Buddhist philosophy, and in some ways I did study that when I was younger, along with a million other things. So I basically you could say I cherry pick whatever I find that resonates with me.

And strangely, because of my job, I am given all kind of future predictions about this, that, and the other thing. But I never internalize that information. I always look inside to see what it is that I'm getting from myself, what is coming through my own filters or connection with Source, and I rely on that to make my decisions in everyday life, going forward.

So you could tell me tomorrow we're going to have – I don't know – a nuclear bomb here where I'm living, and I would listen to you. I might even report it on the front page of my website, if I thought you were a credible whistleblower.

But I wouldn't necessarily do anything about it, unless I got – let's say – a prophetic dream that night or I got a download during the day that just said, "Do this."

Seeing the madness around me, I feel hopeless. Can you suggest some ways that would help me regain trust in the future, and how to act to make a positive change?

I think one of the things is begin to meditate every day. I think that channel meditation and don't be deceived by the word, meditation, because you can ride a train and daydream, and you may be meditating, for all intents and purposes. It's allowing that openness to Source and to the Spirit in all things to come through you.

So it can happen at the most bizarre moments. You can be doing something else, in fact, like running or mowing your lawn or whatever it is people do with their normal lives, driving a car. And all of a sudden, information will come to you, and instead of discounting that information and saying, "Oh well, that was just a daydream or that, you know." Take it seriously, whatever it is. In other words, it doesn't mean it's true, okay?

I had someone recently tell me [something]. Well, I have strong sense that this person is lying. And they were unequivocal about it – that was what they got, and that's what they think is the reality.

And I say, "Look, it doesn't mean your filter is accurate, because it takes years and years of working with yourself and your – whatever you want to call it – resonance filter – that sense of knowing when you're right and when you're wrong and realizing the difference and realizing when you're getting a false story, because something is coming in, sending you down the wrong track, as opposed to a clear channel. This is true of channelers, as well. A lot of channelers do not recognize the difference. So they end up getting taken over by grays and various other negative ET's. They may start out as a clear channel or a fairly clear channel, and have good information, but somewhere in the church or factory, they go off, and they don't realize they've gone off. And then they start feeding humanity a lot of lies.

So there are negative ET's that have a vested interest in taking channels offline. So it is very important to be able to discern truth from falsity, what you should do at any given moment in any given time. But I do believe that it's possible to find your way through that labyrinth. And meditation is one of the best ways, and beginning to listen and get information from Source, and then test it to see if it does prove correct.

So you almost have to have an observer mode towards your own self, and a scientific method towards your own self, such that you listen to the information you get – know that it's coming from somewhere and start to discern when it is correct when it isn't – why it might be infiltrated. Why you might be infiltrated at that time, getting wrong information, and it does take years to perfect. I've been doing this all my life. And more and more as time goes on, I'm right. Way more than I'm wrong. That's all I can say.

So what can I say about that. If I thought something today and it proved true tomorrow, I begin to trust my inner self, my inner knowing, and it's absolutely the difference between life and death for a human to trust their own inner knowing. And to learn to trust that inner knowing even though you're being programmed since birth – you're being programmed in everyday life by things like fluorescent lights and bad food and bad air and bad water and bad this, and bad that.

But you can purify all of that and cleanse all of that. Because you are strong in all of it. You are that... this amazing vehicle that we inhabit has far more powers than we give it credit for.

The way I can persuade someone who has that kind of frame of mind that you're describing, is to basically look at what they do to control you right now. And I say this all the time when I speak in front of groups. If you were easy to control, they would have already programmed you and thrown away the key, the way you would a cow in a pasture.

But they haven't done that. What they have to do, if they have to program you once, and then do it again and do it again and do it again and they have to do it constantly. They have to constantly have the fluorescent lights, constantly have the bad food, constantly give you the television with a lot of crap in it and programming. They have to beam you with programming waves. Then they have to chemtrail you with chemicals. I mean they have to try so hard to keep you under control. You have to look at that and then they have to watch everything you say and do. And when they have an artificial intelligence they direct it to watch everything you say and do – how and why, because it has to learn from you, because we are the teachers. And they can't control us and they want to know what's going to happen in the future, but the only way they can know that is by watching you.

So who's on top? Them or you? You are. You're in the driver's seat. And that's the big you, meaning all of us. That and Source. I mean, because we are all in my view pieces of Source in us.

So that being the case, there is no greater power, we are everything. Source is everything. So just do the math I guess. And what does it come down to? It comes down to even when you're in the worst of all possible places on the planet – meaning your human vehicle is in the way, your spirit is going to surmount and transcend, and your soul is going to continue, even if you die. So there's no point in killing yourself, because you continue anyway. It's just nonsense – you can't be killed. You are eternal.

So with this knowledge, when you start to tap into this, it's not just words on paper. It is actually internalizing it and understanding that this is what should be motivating you to go through your life. You start tapping into it, so when you open yourself to an idea, the idea has power. And the power will come into you, and using that power, you can then move things in the world.

I can say that's the essence of magic, this is what the Illuminati use. You can learn all of this. And it's only you that's keeping you back ultimately.

If you buy into what they are trying to sell you, just don't buy it anymore.

If you could plant one seed in the mainstream mind, what would that be?

Get the truth out. *Get the truth out there.* Tell everyone the truth. Make the world aware of your truth and of the gifts. Reveal your gifts to the world. Don't hide your gifts, as they say, under a bushel or whatever that is. Don't hide your light. You are all brighter if you shine your light. Okay, it's obvious and that's what we need, we need people to stop hiding. Stop covering up who they truly are.

Because with your true self comes gifts and all our gifts are different and who would not see the wisdom in that. That's like the ultimate creator's wisdom to have every individual have its own unique gift, whether it be an animal, a plant, a human, whatever, that would shine, make it all the brighter. So we don't have the same gifts. But shine yours for the world, because that is how you give back to the world, by shining and sharing who you are. So don't hide.

The future is
not something
we enter
The future
is something
we create

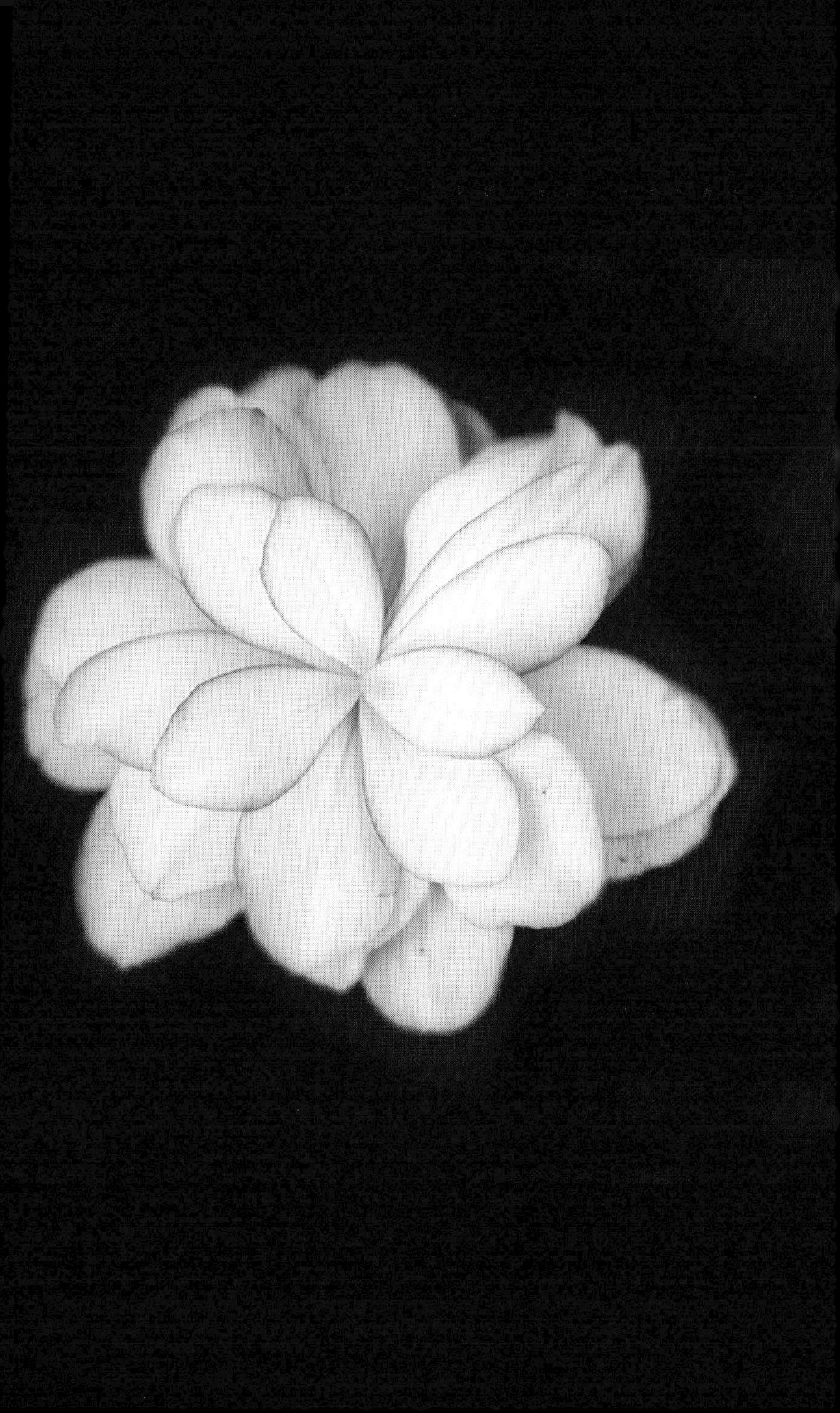

OLE DAMMEGÅRD

Ole Dammegård

OLE DAMMEGÅRD

Introduction

For many years investigator Ole Dammegård has been on a quest to find the truth behind some of the darkest conspiracies in the history of world – such as the murders of US President John F. Kennedy, Robert Kennedy, Martin Luther King Jr., Swedish Prime Minister Olof Palme, John Lennon, the mass shootings in the US and in Norway, the blowing up of m/s Estonia killing at least 852 innocent people, and countless black operations, including Charlie Hebdo and the Copenhagen Shootings.

Ole Dammegård has made hundreds of international interviews and is totally dedicated to revealing the New World Order's agenda including False Flag-operations all over the world. He often says he is not here to spread fear; instead his goal is to prevent the 'Global Elite' from turning this beautiful planet into a controlled and fearful place.

*We all deserve so much better –
it's time to stop the madness and
heal the world with love.*

www.lightonconspiracies.com

When did you start exploring your field, was there a specific event that led you to this path of waking up?

For me it began around 1983-84. One night when I was visiting a friend in Stockholm they showed a documentary about the J.F.K. assassination. That was the first time I ever saw the so-called Zapruder film where a bystander called Abraham Zapruder filmed the whole assassination of J.F.K. and where you can very clearly see that the final gruesome head shot comes from the front and to the right – where the so-called grassy knoll area is – not from the area, where the alleged killer, Harvey Oswald, is said to have been up in the Texas School Book Depository.

It is so obvious for anyone with any kind of brain activity. This is based on normal physics that the shot came from a totally different direction, thus making the official story an absolute lie. For me it was a shocking experience, because that was the first time ever that I felt the impact of these lies.

The big question of it all was when I saw this in the early eighties twenty years after the assassination. It was still being pumped out by these major news corporations as the official story being the truth. So I was just dumbfounded about how these big companies push these very obvious lies unless there's something very big behind it.

That was the thing that really started my interest in this area. Up until then I had been very interested in spiritual books. but also books about conspiracies the Wild West, historical books, and so on. But that was the one that really ignited the flame that sparked the whole thing.

From then on I read a couple hundred books about the J.F.K. assassination that then got me into the assassination of Robert Kennedy, which is also a conspiracy where I even found some of the same people involved. That also took me into the area of the Martin Luther King assassination, Malcolm X, even Abraham Lincoln. The more I dug into it. the more this area just opened up and up and up. So many of these so-called events, these awful events that have changed world history, have been shown to be connected.

I'm talking about the exact same people being involved in many of these events. So instead of looking at a crazy world with a lot of political assassinations done by lone crazy guys all over the place, I have been able to find direct links showing that so much mayhem in this world is being created by a very few elite people. Well, they call themselves the elite. I would call them the minority or the few.

But that very few people in key positions are behind a lot of awful stuff in this world, giving me great hope as well because that also makes it so much easier to handle, and limits the problem to a small group that we need to transcend to get to the next level.

How do you see the world today in the terms of the challenges facing us?

It's a very challenging time. It's also a very exciting time that we're living in. It's like we're being pushed into a corner, and being attacked from all different directions. Most people are not even aware that there is a real war going on against humanity. It's being thrown at us from all different directions, through food, air, vaccines, GMO's, wars, financial mayhem, false flag operations, political assassinations, and so on.

The thing is that most people are not aware of the details. So many of us are feeling very strongly that something very wrong is going on in the world. This is something that helps many people wake up to the fact that, '… something odd is going on, something very weird is going on, and I need to take a step forward to start informing myself to get the power back and really understand what is going on.'

So I've devoted some thirty years of my life to expose what I see as the real truth, to focus on totally fearless exposure of this small group. By aiming the spotlight at them, we will be able to expose their methods in a totally nonviolent way, and see if we can get one step ahead of them, instead of always being ones that are behind. I'm convinced that we will be able to solve this and take the step to the next level of a beautiful future.

Ole Dammegård

Does it matter if we vote or not?

During my whole life I've never voted, because at a very early age I found out that the elections don't really mean a lot in most countries. This so-called power elite that is behind what is called the New World Order are on a totally different level. So what we are seeing with these elections are like a theatre play.

Most countries have the same political system based on the two different parties: one called left, one called right, and then you got a central party or some small parties in the middle, giving the illusion of democracy, an illusion of freedom of choice. So it's just based on the same thing.

When they start going into politics, many of the politicians have a pure heart, pure intentions, and they really want to make a difference in life. But the higher up you get in the ranks in these areas, the more corrupt it gets. So once you get up to the level where we're talking like elections for a conference, more or less all of them are totally corrupt now.

It's very sad to say but I think so. Nowadays these elections are very staged events. So it is by studying groups like the Bilderberg group and Council on Foreign Relations – these types of groups – where you will see where the real selection is taking place, where people are being selected to the next term for president or prime minister. We are being served an illusion of an election where the different candidates are just different arms of the same body. So it doesn't really matter which one we will choose. It will still be the same power structure behind it that just moves forward.

This is also why there are no changes in the world. We see the same just repeating, repeating, because it's the same power structure and we're just being played. So take the power back by not giving it away to the government.

When you actually look at it, it is right there in front of us telling us what's really going on. They are playing us, and it's time for us to pull away the curtain and see what's going on, then take our power back by awakening to the real truth to see that maybe we don't even need governments.

Maybe we are at a point in history where it's time for us to follow the rules of the heart. It's part of our structure that we have a very silent voice in our heart that will tell us what is right and what is wrong. The more we listen to that voice, the more we choose the right thing, the road of love where one chooses options of not hurting or damaging anyone and having respect for everything around you, including nature and people, your fellow neighbors, your neighboring countries.

The more we choose love instead of hate and fear, the more this world will come back into a state of balance, where there is no need for this government – or control tool – that the government is now. Why? Because governments have taken over. They were there to serve us to do our will, but nowadays they are the ones controlling us. We don't even know what's going on, because they have turned the whole thing around.

Now they're ruling from behind closed doors with all of these rules of so-called national security – absolute b.s. – national security is their security – the people hiding in the dark. It's their security – all of this top secret security of the nation and all of these ways of stopping information from getting out. It's only there to control the information that will leak out about them and their actions.

National security should be transparency. It's through transparency that we can understand what is going on. Nobody else is diverting and manipulating us. This has to stop. We have to start seeing what is actually going.

One great way would be to have something like the Formula One drivers have on their overalls: all these labels of the different companies that sponsor them. With the government and the people working in government, if they had the same type of system where we could see exactly who is funding them, that would make it a totally different game. Then we would see what's going on.

When it comes to voting... maybe it's okay on a local level where people have still not become corrupt, where they are still pure, their intention is still pure, that would be the area where I would maybe considering voting. Other than that, when it comes to prime minister or president, that is just a big joke.

Nowadays they want all the voting to be digital, meaning that they can totally manipulate the whole thing. It's just totally out of order and out of control now. For instance, the second term of George Bush Jr. was a total fraud. It was found out and people knew about it, and they still just continued. He still sat for another four years, and everybody was like dumbfounded, but that's the way they do. They have no respect for us at this point. It's time for us to show them that we're here to be respected.

What are your thoughts about money and the global banks?

Money the biggest joke of all, the biggest hoax, and the biggest control tool ever seen. It is when you start seeing how money is created out of thin air, and how it's used to totally enslave us. It is just incredible.

I started waking up to the fact about how money was being used in the nineties after meeting David Icke. I started to understand the banking system. It's just incredible how we have been letting them control us in this way.

Because most people are not aware of how this money thing works. If you want to, I can just give you a quick sketch of how the whole system is set up:

What is needed is a central bank. You need to control a central bank in a country, so that all banks in that country are connected to that central bank. That is essential for this whole conspiracy to work. What they do then is to set up rules, so that, for instance, if a bank has ten thousand in their bank vault, then they can lend out a hundred thousand. If they have ten percent, they can lend out one hundred percent of that – on top sort of what they actually have. So you go to your bank and say, "I want to buy a house, or I want to buy a car." They would then look at you, saying "... but can we really trust you? Are you somebody we can rely on" You say, "Yes, I promise I'm a good guy." They say then, in the and, "Okay, if you are a good guy, then we will accept you. But we will need your property as security if you cannot pay." You would then say. "Yeah, of course. No problem," because you know you will pay. You're an honest, decent guy.

I'm not saying that people working in the bank system are aware of this on a low level – it's totally compartmentalized so that the lower down in the power pyramid you are in the banking system, the less you know. That is made like that by design. The higher up you go, that's where people become more aware of these things.

So they say that you need a loan for a hundred thousand. Since they have ten thousand dollars in the back vault. Of that they can – according to rules – lend out a hundred thousand dollars. But this is not in cash. You will very rarely be given that in cash. It would be as a check or nowadays just digital. They go on the keyboard, and what is *said* to be hundred thousand dollars goes into your bank account.

You then meet up with the owner of the property you're going to buy. You give them the check, and say, "Thank you very much. Here is the check for a hundred thousand cash. Now please give me the keys to the property." You do that. The old owner then, because he's very aware of that, thinks, "Oh my god, this check can be stolen." He then goes to his bank – whatever bank it is, it's still connected to the central bank – and gives them this check and says, "Please put this in my account, so that it's safe." That hundred thousand dollars is then put in his account, meaning that the bank – whatever bank it is – is then allowed to lend out ten percent of the whole amount that the bank now is allowed to lend out to someone else.

And so your going in there, the bank having ten thousand dollars in the bank vault, your asking for a loan gives them the right to – out of thin air, just from a touch on the keyboard – get an additional ninety thousand out of thin air and put it into your account. This money did not exist just a few minutes ago. Boom, suddenly it's there. And since, then it is given to the former owner of the property who then goes to the bank and puts it in his account, giving that bank the ability to add another ninety percent of that amount.

Ninety percent of that amount then just continues and continues... and all the time, the money is created out of thin air.

Many countries have also set it up so that every time money is printed, it's printed on debt. So that the taxpayers have to pay for it to receive the money notes, meaning that every time a new dollar or euro is printed, it's printed and creates debt for the population, meaning that we will never ever be able to get out of debt. It will just keep building, building... in all countries.

This is also the explanation of how every single country in the world is so buried in debt. Because normally, how could a country – like the U.S. who is giving out money or lending out money in the billions to different to other countries – how can they do that when they themselves are in so much debt?

If the system was the way we think it is and the way it's supposed to be, that would not be possible. Only countries with a lot of money could lend it out to other countries. But here it's created out of thin air, and that's the big hoax.

I hope I explained it in a way that is understandable. If not, whoever reads this please start studying this yourself. Understand what's going on, because this is controlling your life, my life, and our lives on a level that is just absolutely incredible.

What do you think about the debt-based economy people are stuck in, and is there a way out?

This is more or less what I've just explained, it's an absolute hoax – the biggest tool of slavery in the history of mankind – and most of us are not even aware of it. So it is very, very important to become aware of.

And also see that more and more people are starting to study this and are finding ways of getting out of this.

The whole taxing system is also in some countries totally illegal. For instance, in the US there is absolutely no law that says that the normal person has to pay income tax. That is just taken out of thin air and pushed on the population. Everybody has just been bending down and saying, "Yes, yes, of course I'm a good person. I will then pay tax because that is what is needed of me as a decent member of society." But there is no rule, no law in the US stating that a person has to pay income tax, and more and more people have become aware of this.

There was even one man a few years ago who put in a whole page ad in *The New York Times* or *Washington Post* saying, "I hereby offer fifty thousand dollars to anyone who can show me where that law is. Point out the law and you win fifty thousand dollars." No one has ever found it. Agents of the I.R.S. Are more and more also waking up to the fact ro what is going on and have turned whistleblowers. They are now doing everything they can to expose this massive hoax that is just strangling people financially.

When it comes to money this area is the head of the snake. Iit's the one that is strangling us pushing our head down in the mud on a level that is just incredible, and keeping us enslaved through a whole life.

They've also set it up now so that they will get people as quickly as possible into the so-called system with student loans. So before you even had your education, you are in debt that will take you a lifetime to get out of sometimes.

It's time for us to understand how we are being played, how we are being manipulated, and then put a stop to it just by saying no, refusing to be part of it and then aiming the spotlight right at them, exposing their methods and just saying enough is enough.

We have started to read and hear about microchipping people. What does that mean?

This has been around for such a long time. I know David Icke was one of the first ones who really started warning about this in the 1990s saying that it's coming, it's coming. The whole idea is to connect everything into this global computer where everything can be totally controlled from all different areas of life including you and your body – where you are, what you do, everything. The way into that is through this chip that they want us to have.

They started with these missing children campaigns in the U.S. where there was big propaganda saying – on milk cartons and so on – find this missing child, find this missing child. Then saying in the background more and more that if you could microchip your child, then we could find the child and see the location of the child at any time. Then we would be able to stop these awful things. They did it with dogs and cats to get our minds used to the idea that this is a great idea. And it is a great idea, if it's done in a human way, in a way that helps humanity. It could be a great tool.

But their plan, their agenda – the people that are behind this once – again the so-called New World Order – their agenda is very, very dark. The microchip is very central in the whole plan and that plan is to totally control all the areas of our lives through that chip. So that they can connect us to a computer, they can track us with G.P.S. so that they can see where we are at all times. They can totally control and see what our finances are, like how we're using our money, where we're working.

I would say the microchip is a major threat, a major threat to freedom. I would stay away from this as far as I could. For sure do not let them do anything to your kids or loved ones when it comes to this area.

In Sweden and other countries people are very much into gadgets and think it's so cool with everything. They've introduced the microchipping in a way that it sounds really cool. You can get into the VIP section of these nightclubs. If you use that, you can open your door without a key. You can pay without having to you pick up your wallet. But the implications of doing that by a microchip is just incredible, because once the chip is in your body, then whoever controls the microchip through the wireless computer access can do so many things with this chip without you knowing it.

So I would very much recommend anyone to stay far away from this as far away as possible.

What are your thoughts about depopulation?

I wish I could say that it's absolute fantasies and conspiracy theories. But when you study the history and the background of the people in the so-called New World Order, one of the parts of their plan is to depopulate this planet. They want to eliminate about two-thirds of us, then use what is left as a slave population. It sounds absolutely horrific, it sounds like it's taken out of a very dark science fiction movie, but that is what has come out more and more in documents leaking out.

You can also see it in things like what is called Agenda 21, where they very openly describe their plan. And their plan is to eliminate a lot of us. I mean kill a lot of us. I don't think it's up to them to play God. Nature has to have its own way.

If they want to eliminate people, well, they can eliminate themselves. That would be a blessing in many ways. It's not right for them to decide who should live and who should die.

Their plan is indirect murder... absolutely not okay.

What is your opinion on vaccines? Are vaccinations part of the depopulation question?

It is indeed and vaccines, I cannot emphasis enough, are tool of horror – absolute horror. These vaccines are part of the depopulation agenda that is also part of making absolutely billions of money for them. When you look into how this whole thing has been set up, they create these virus scares like – if you remember – the swine flu scare, where the whole world was being freaked out. This awful, awful swine flu is coming, it's coming, its going to kill us all.

I ask you, how many dead people did you see? This was on a pandemic level of alert that was globally higher than ever before. How many people did you see die? How many people were stumbling around in the streets with big boils on their face and rotten bodies? Absolute no one.

The swine flu? Absolute hoax. It was a massive hoax. The whole idea was to get people to take the vaccines. They always use this old Roman template, Problem-Reaction-Solution, when it comes to these things.

Here they say, "Oh, it's the swine flu. Oh, it's Ebola," and I don't know the next one they gonna come up with, maybe it's the upside-down green monkey virus or a blown-up camel virus or whatever they're going to come up with as a stupid name... to freak us out so we would say, "Oh my God. Oh, my God. I need a solution," and the solution they present us with is the vaccine. But these vaccines are theirs and manufactured to destroy our immune system totally and not in one go.

It's very important for them that we will not be able to track down, go backwards, and track the evidence to the vaccines. So what they have done is they made cocktails that will interact inside your body once it's in there. Then wait for a while and then it explodes from the inside, totally knocking you out.

So I would strongly suggest that many, many of the physical problems that especially young people are having nowadays with A.D.H.D and all of these different letter combinations and allergies, many forms of weird diseases, weird symptoms, are directly connected to these awful vaccines.

They have a lot of mercury, formaldehyde, and dead bodies and so on that are the things that bypass all the natural security walls, the firewalls in the body, such as the skin, all the different layers in the skin that are there to protect your inner system. And here, through that needle you just bypass all of them in one go. Then whatever you pump in the body has no defence.

Ole Dammegård

When you look back in history like – for instance, one of the companies that is very central in the spreading of these awful virus scares is a company called C.D.C., the Center for Disease Control. based in Atlanta, Georgia in the U.S. It was founded in 1946, the very same year when Operation Paperclip was very active, when they exported lots of Nazi scientists from Nazi Germany into the U.S. and other countries.

One of the companies that started using their knowledge was the C.D.C. So here we have Nazi scientists that come directly from doing a lot of experiments on human beings being employed by this company that since then has been involved in so many of these awful diseases and they're the ones that own the patent of, for instance, the ebola virus. They've been directly involved in the creation of the AIDS virus as well, and the swine flu virus was connected to the C.D.C.

Go to their website. You can read about it. It's just incredible. Together and in conjunction with the C.D.C. you have these big companies, Big Pharma companies, that are producing these vaccines. These vaccines are made most of the time with no control. They have no idea what's going to happen. There's no guarantee that nothing bad will not happen. And they've taken away by law you cannot sue these companies anymore if anything happens to you.

So vaccines are just horrific and just the thought that nowadays some children before the age of two have been pumped with 26 different vaccines. I just want to cry when I think of it.

We have never given any of our kids any vaccines and they are super strong. These beautiful children that we've been blessed with are never sick. Maybe three days in their whole life in total. When you compare with their friends that had the vaccines. They have all kinds of allergies and they are so weak and with AHD, and all of these kinds of strange diagnoses.

There's one man that I would very much recommend you to study if you're interested in this: Dr. Leonard Horowitz. Very early in the 80s he started exposing what was going on. He confronted people being part of creating the AIDS virus – Dr. Robert Gallo and other people – totally exposing what they've done, how they were financed by military interest and the money that they were being given to create these viruses.

He has made one documentary that you can find on YouTube. It's called, *In Lies We Trust,* which is an absolute incredibly good title,l because that is what it's all about.

Listen to Dr. Leonard Horowitz. Listen to when he goes through what's in these vaccines. That will give you a good understanding of what's actually going on in that area.

What are GMOs?

GMOs are genetically modified organisms. These things that you're asking me about – they're all connected. They are very scary areas to get into. The whole idea, the official story is that GMOs – genetically modified organisms – are there to save and help humanity.

Turn it around. It's absolute the opposite.

There's a one company called Monsanto which is an evil on this planet. It personifies the word evil. It should be called Mondiablo or something like that. It was founded in 1901 by a man called John Francis Queeny. He was actually a member of the Knights of Malta. But he was married to a woman called Olga Mendes Monsanto – that's where the name came from. Their first product was the chemical saccharin, the artificial sweetener that was actually sold to Coca-Cola. Coca-Cola and companies like Disney have helped support the development of this company, Monsanto.

When you look at Monsanto, it has been one of the world's biggest chemical producers. They have done aspirin and other things that most people have used. They were part of developing Agent Orange, which was a chemical warfare product that was used in the Vietnam War to make all the jungle plants lose their leaves so the Vietcong couldn't hide.

But it produced massive bodily harm to the population, all kinds of deformations, babies being born with severely dysfunctional bodies, absolutely horrendous.

But Monsanto was also very much involved in the Manhattan Project where they created the atomic bomb which was later dropped on both Hiroshima and Nagasaki, killing hundreds of thousands of Japanese. So it's a company with a very deadly and dark background.

They came up with the idea to produce pesticides – especially one product that is called Roundup – that are spread out into 130 countries all over the world now. What they've done with that pesticide is they've started to create these GMOs which are genetically modified organisms where they added things in the organism itself. They put themselves in God's role and started playing around with his creation, creating monster plants and absolutely horrific stuff.

One of their ideas is to create plants that can resist all types of problems, that can resist draft, that can resist aluminum, that can resist different attacks. But these plants themselves are toxic. Some of the plants even give out pesticides to the plant itself, then that is now being presented to us as food.

What is the logic of eating pesticides that are so toxic? The more you start looking into GMOs and look at the official web sites, it all looks beautiful, it is there to save us and that's the solution for the future. But then when you look who is in the boardrooms, who are behind all of these things, we get back to the same people who are very central to what is called the New World Order.

Hillary Clinton is on the board. You've got Donald Rumsfeld. George Bush Sr. is very central to this whole thing, helping this company to get bigger and bigger access into the global food reserve.

One of the things they do is to create plants that can resist, for instance, chemtrail droppings – these chemicals coming from the sky that kill normal plants. But we are back to the Problem-Reaction-Solution. The problem: the plants die. Our reaction: "Oh, my God. We need protection. We need a solution." Then they serve us the solution: their GMO plants, where they are the owners of the patent, meaning that they control it.

One of the things they've also done is to create terminator seeds. Like plants, tomato plants and many others that look beautiful, they're fantastic plants. But the thing is, there are no seeds. It's a one-season plant. It grows. It gives you the harvest, the vegetable, then it dies, meaning that for the next year's crop, you need to buy their seeds once again.

They've bought up massive amount of seed and manipulated so many plants where they own the patent.

The idea for them is to control as much of the world's food production as possible through their seeds, but without any guarantees on what it's doing to our health. More studies are showing that it is dangerous and very bad for us – what is coming from these GMOs.

Nowadays they're spending billions defeating state and federal legislations, going around different laws and rules. They don't even have to show if there are GMOs in different foods. So it's very hard, we don't even know what we are eating nowadays.

These seeds spread naturally from fields to big areas through the wind and now they're suing a lot of farmers, especially in the US, where they find GMO plants in their fields. They sue the farmer saying, "You are using this without our allowance." And then that will then knock out that farmer. Then they can take over that farm as well.

We are back to a massive scheme of manipulation aiming for total control in all different areas of life. Food, air, water, you name it, finances, and so on. They're trying to control us and the GMOs are one major block in this war that they're trying to build around us.

Do chemtrails exist, and if so, how would you describe them?

I'm very sorry to say, yes, once again, yes, they exist big time. Chemtrails are contrary to what people normally think when they see a jet plane. They see this white coming after it, called a contrail, its condensation trail. At a certain altitude and at a certain temperature the water coming from the jet engine turns into ice crystals, and that is what we can see on a clear blue day. Sometimes you can see this condensation trail follows the jet plane in the sky.

But chemtrails is a totally different story. Chemtrails consist of chemicals that are being sprayed out. The difference is you can see these trails when the planes come. They leave a long, long very white stripe across the sky. Then that stripe will slowly, slowly spread out and in the end, if it's, for instance, here in southern Spain where the sky is naturally blue many days of the year. It is very obvious for us to see them. It's much easier to see them here than in many other countries where there are lots of clouds. But you can see when they do chemtrail spraying on an intense day here.

It starts off before dawn, maybe 6:30 in the morning. You will see the first plane comes and leaves a long white stripe. Then about twelve minutes later there's another diagonal stripe, another plane coming, then twelve fifteen minutes later, a third plane comes, and a fourth, and a fifth plane. Then they return further inland, doing the same thing. So you get a carpet of stripes that slowly, slowly disappear into the air. It dissolves into the air.

Then after four or five hours of these planes going across the sky, the whole skies is one white haze – chemical toxic sky. It's awful to see and most people don't even react. It's incredible, because it's so big, and the magnitude of it all just so big that people cannot grasp it. If a truck went through one of the towns here and let out that amount of exhausts, he would be stopped within thirty seconds. The police would just totally seize the truck and put him in jail and fine him.

But since it's so big, it's like you cannot see it. The first time I became aware of this was in 2008. I went out openly talking about this on a radio station here called Talk Radio Europe. I together with radio host Steve Gilmore did everything we could to expose many of these things that we're talking about here like chemtrails, vaccines, the global elite, the political assassinations. In one way chemtrails are a blessing in disguise, because it is one of the things that is so obvious once you see them. They're so visible. So once you start seeing what's going on you cannot deny it anymore.

Most of the other things we're talking about here are behind closed doors, their so-called conspiracies theories. But this, once you start seeing it, there's no denial. It's just so obvious.

If I can just jump back to the GMOs. I just want to say that what I think is so wonderful in this world is that wherever there is a problem, there's also solutions. According to people like Ken Rohla who's a specialist in many of these areas, there is a way of reversing the GMO effect.

He recommends a website called www.restandrepair.com/microbe-blast/, especially one product they called microbe blast. This solution, once you feed it to the plants, goes into – for instance the apples or whatever it is – that's been GMO-manipulated and restores the DNA, so it resets it and gets it back to the way nature was supposed to have created it.

So this is a wonderful thing that I hope will be more and more open to and available for normal people.

Please share your thoughts about the environment and the current weather conditions.

With the chemtrails we've been talking about, which consist to a main extent of aluminum, barium, strontium, to some extent arsenic, one of the things it does when it's sprayed out in the amount that we are talking about, tons and tons and tons of it come down and changes the pH of the soil, making it very acidic. When the soul goes acidic, this really affects the plants, so they get weaker and weaker. This is where Monsanto and other companies come in offering us GMOs because they are aluminum resistant.

But the spraying of this also affects our immune system, very much turning our body environment very acidic as well, so that many of the deceases can flourish. Cancer can grow and funguses, so it's very bad for our health as well.

They use chemtrails as a weapon through systems like HAARP technology in combination with chemtrails, where they can use this as a weather control weapon against us. They can create tsunamis, they can create earthquakes, tornados, they can create drought, too much rain. This is what we see, they're totally messing the whole thing up to make the countries where there are already droughts into desert areas. Countries where it rains too much already. like England, are totally drowned instead.

All the time with the idea to weaken us. The idea behind The New World order is to weaken us in all different areas, to make us weaker and weaker, so that they can get bigger and bigger, stronger and stronger, control and totally strangle us.

I hope that one day I'm going to wake up and see that this problem, with so many tons of especially aluminum in the air and in the soil, will suddenly turn out to be a fantastic solution for the world, that thanks to all of this aluminum, we will then be able to do whatever it is… but at this point I cannot see it.

I really think that we should very much let mother earth be the way she is, do everything we can to get her back in balance and give her back her health and stop poisoning her. This weather thing is one thing that we should not manipulate. It really is like mad scientists who have just been sponsored and are going totally wild, not having a clue what they're actually doing.

Do you have a practice that keeps your spirits high?

I do indeed. I'm Raja Yoga teacher. That is a 5000-year-old philosophy that is actually called the science of the mind. I have this fantastic teacher. Her name is Nalanie Harilela Chellaram. Through that knowledge and the ways that they recommend through these Scriptures, how to control the mind, how to calm you down, how to choose love instead of fear, many, many areas of life have really helped me a lot.

Also my sweetheart and I often sit and watch the sunset. We have some chickens and a duck, and just sitting there with them, you know, sitting cuddling a chicken and just listening to the sounds of nature, watching the horses, feeling the gentle breeze on your face, these types of things, getting back in balance. I always walk barefoot. That helps ground me. And the more I focus on not letting fear into my mind, the better I feel and the more of a difference I can make to the world.

So I focus very much on not getting into fear mode, not getting into anger, revenge, hate, these feelings, but not closing my eyes to what's going on, on the contrary, entering into these very dark areas with a very open heart and an open mind. Just see that this is part of this divine game that we are in and for some reason apparently we have to be in this very extreme situation at the moment. I don't know why, but we are there, so we just have to deal with it. So I'm very grateful for Nalanie, who has helped me see and enter into this stage in a loving way, in a way that spreads no fear, but spreads hope and love.

I also meditate every day, or more or less every day. I try to be aware of my breathing, because I know when I get scared or if I get worried, I only breathe very high up in the chest. So I focus on getting the breath down. Take ten deep breaths, for instance, and then that calms the body down. When the body calms down, then the mind calms down.

Things like that really help me, and also, to do good, to be kind, to spread kindness really boosts my soul. I love it, and it's a hobby of mine to see wherever I can help, because it makes other people feel good, makes me feel good. So it's a win-win solution.

Seeing the madness around me, I feel hopeless. Can you suggest some ways that would help me regain my trust in the future and how to act to make a positive change?

I think most people who are in the process of awakening go through different periods. It's almost like when you've lost a loved one. First, you are in total denial. You cannot accept that what you see is actually true. You try to defend and say, "No, no, no, it cannot be true." But then the more evidence that is put forward in front of you and the more you start seeing this is actually happening, then many people go into despair, depression, anger, and so on.

It's totally natural, but not the way to go. The way forward is to see if we can let go of these negative emotions, because they don't help anyone. They just add to the problem. The more you can become aware of how your brain works and your thoughts, then you can also become aware that you're not a slave unto your thoughts, but that you can actually control them. Your mind is able to think only one thought at a time. So if it starts thinking a negative thought, you can just swap it for a good one, to a more positive one. And the more you train to do that when these dark thoughts enter, you can get yourself back in balance.

Also meditation would help you calm down the mind. Once again not to see what's going on, but to be able to deal with these things in a balanced way, where you can make decisions based on not coming from fear, but a balanced awakened choice of how to deal with things.

The power structure is behind all of this darkness. They focus on divide-and-conquer. They want us to fear each other. They want us to see each other as enemies, they want ourselves to be very selfish, just think about I, me, mine, my family, everybody else can just sod off.

One way of working against them or for us would be to look around and see where I can make a difference, how I can help, who I can help, who I can join up with. The more you become aware of your thoughts and the way you look upon other people, the more you can let go of judgment and anger or fear and hate and focus more on looking lovingly on your fellow human beings. That in itself is a major step forward, because that changes the whole world around you. It changes people around you as well.

Some people say to me, "Yeah, but that's just too big. I can't change my mind like that." In those cases I would recommend that you look at a normal day. If you start dividing it into small little chapters, for instance, I wake up, okay, when I wake up, then focus on my thoughts. Are they positive or negative about the day? How do I see when I look upon my family? Do I see them or am I just entered in a daze.

See if you can become aware of that, and then as much as possible choose to be in the moment, and be in what is called love when you look upon people, when you talk to people. Then once you wake up, you eat breakfast. Focus on the breakfast, focus on tasting it, focus on appreciating it. Be grateful that you have food on the table.

Then maybe you have to take the car and go somewhere, that is like a new chapter where you can once again focus on when you're in the car. Treat the people around you with care and respect and other people in the traffic. When you're in the car, you're also have to focus very much on safety. So don't sit and space out.

Then every time you meet someone, every time you do something, see that as a new chapter and see in this chapter, of this meeting, or this phone call, or whatever it is. Focus on these minutes: let me see if I can manage to focus on love in this situation.

I would recommend the more times you manage to go in the love way instead of the fear or hate way, the better your life will become, and also the more creative you will become, the more you will affect people around you in a positive way that can help lift this world to the next level.

If you could plant one seed in the mainstream mind, what would that be?

Focus on love. Focus on love in all different situations.

There are some experiments that I love. It's like love is in this universe what we call the highest frequency of them all. I'm not talking about love, the physical love, or being in love, but the love that can make a mother pull off a car from her child in a car crash, or make a father just jump into a burning house to save his family.

That type of love has an incredible power. That is what is labelled in this universe as the highest of the high of frequencies. It's higher than the frequency of thought. The lowest of the low is pure terror, absolute fear. That is very, very low, if not the lowest in the universe. If you take a high frequency and a low frequency in a laboratory and let the two meet, what happens is not that they start struggling, and then after a while they end up in the middle, like fifty-fifty in the gray zone, and that's where they meet each other and they can get along. No, the lower frequency just gets annulled. It disappears, and it's miraculous to see.

When I see people like Jesus or Buddha, I see them as super hackers. They cracked the code to the matrix. They saw that, whatever the problem is, meet it with a higher frequency. I think that is what Jesus is saying. I'm not a religious person, but this is my understanding. He said whatever the problem is understand that they do not know what they're doing. And the way out is to meet it with a higher frequency. While you're at it, why not with the highest, meet it with love.

So, if you can manage to, focus on love. There is this magic thing that just – boom – diffuses this dark force. I've seen it in situations in war zones and I've had the privilege of experiencing it myself when being approached by people in uniform, people trying to really scare me, waving with weapons.

The thing that really works for me is the word *divine*. If I have somebody standing in front of me angry or screaming or threatening me, if I turn down the volume, so I don't hear the words, and focus on his or her face, then keep repeating, keep my mind in love mode, just keep repeating the word *divine, divine, divine,* he is somebody's son, he is somebody's brother, and he is somebody's father, *divine, divine,* he does not know what he does, keep repeating that, almost like a mantra – that keeps my mind out of fear mode. Because if I get into fear, then the chances of me getting hurt or someone else getting hurt is a lot bigger.

The times that I manage to stay in that frequency of love and not being freaked out, then a minute or so down the line, suddenly you can see the spark in the other o, ts eye. The whole situation diffuses the person who is trying to intimidate you.

The person who is normally used to people just bending over, being very scared of their uniform, or whatever it is, or their title. When they meet someone where there's no fear, where there's no judgment, where there's only love, they get very confused, and after a while, if you do not buy into it, too, it's like defusing a bomb, and then suddenly something happens.

I would say very, very often the situation turns into something totally different. Instead of a very threatening situation, suddenly you're standing talking together.

I've seen it with SWAT teams or police, for instance, people that have been sent out seeing me as a modern day terrorist. When I do not buy into fear then after a few minutes suddenly they are so friendly. They're so nice they offer to help, they give me their business card, and "Here's my private number, if you need any assistance." They are absolutely incredible.

So whatever the situation is, *focus on love*.

From Ole's solo album **From Prison To Paradise** (1997):

Once upon a time in a place not far from here
There were so much loneliness, despair and oh so much fear
Darkness ruled all over the land, there was lightning in the Sky
Causing wars and separation with no one knowing why

These evil times raised leaders disguised as Kind and True
Hiding the Truth in misty fog so only very few people knew
Controlled by an Elite few manipulating you and me
Closing out the Light and Power that can make us all be free

Wake up! Wake up! We've gotta wake up! Now

Forced by invisible powers, demanded to conform
Into shapes unknown to Mankind making him totally abnormal
Drowned in debts and sorrows blaming others for their lot
Made Man believe to be inferior, feeling tiny like a dot

But then came Times of Change covering countries and their towns
Few became many and soon the prison walls came down
Starting with the men in the mirrors staring right back into their eyes
Understanding that this was a chance to stop those hideous lies

Unhappiness is merely an Illusion of misery
Based on brainwash and a misconception of True Reality
From now on let's build bridges between our Souls and Hearts
So we together can rejoice when the final change comes to its start

Now let us wake up! We've gotta wake up! We've gotta wake up!

Turning prison into Paradise may seem too much to achieve
But believe me, it only takes One Strong Spirit to be Free
The True Power of a pyramid is never at the top
Instead, it is We The People that can make this global game stop
Did you get it?

Wake up – Wake up – we've gotta wake up – It has to stop.

Truth is available only to those who have the courage to question whatever they have been taught

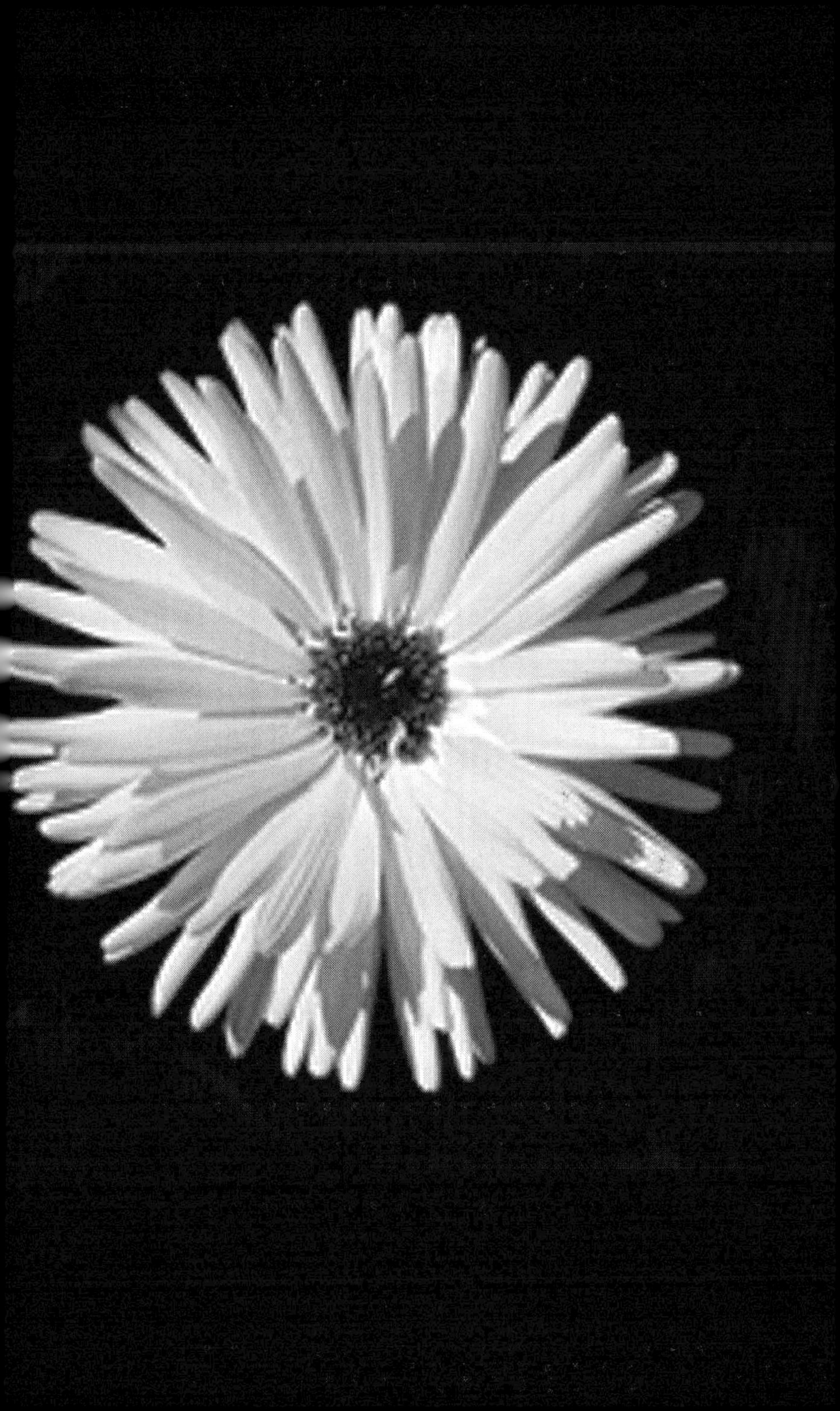

KEVIN BARRETT

Kevin Barrett

KEVIN BARRETT

Introduction

Dr. Kevin Barrett, a Ph.D. Arabist-Islamologist, is one of America's best-known critics of the War on Terror. Dr. Barrett has appeared many times on Fox, CNN, PBS and other broadcast outlets, and has inspired feature stories and op-eds in the New York Times, the Christian Science Monitor, the Chicago Tribune, and other leading publications.

He holds advanced degrees in English Literature, French Literature, and African Literature. Dr. Barrett has taught at colleges and universities in San Francisco, Paris, and Wisconsin, where he ran for Congress in 2008. He currently works as a non-profit organizer, author, public speaker and talk radio host.

www.truthjihad.com, www.noliesradio.org

When did you start exploring your field, and was there a specific event that led you to this path of waking up?

Well, I've been least half-awake since I was in high school. I believe I was about sixteen when in about 1975 I saw Mark Lane give a talk on the JFK assassination at Marquette University in Milwaukee Wisconsin. During that talk Mark Lane showed a copy of the Zapruder film which had just been released. Nobody had seen them since 1963 and the frames showing the bullet impact on President Kennedy made it very clear that he was being shot from the front. Life magazine showed a depiction of the relevant frames.

The frames were printed in reverse order, which suggested that the president had been shot from behind, as the official story claimed. So after seeing Mark Lane's presentation, which also included a lot of other evidence of a sensational coup d'état in 1963, I realized that there was something deeply wrong, and I did some further investigation, including checking with film experts to find out if there was any way that the reverse frames in Life magazine could have been an accident. I concluded that, no, there was obviously a coup d'état, an assassination of the president, and a cover up that involved the mainstream media.

So I learned that when I was about age 16 and that's been sort of a background assumption of my life since then. [My assumption] has been that we're living in a kind of Orwellian world in which the consensus reality is manufactured by the mainstream media and the oligarchy that owns it is quite different from what's actually going on.

I spent most of my life doing other things not directly devoting myself to activism, except for a brief stint of one year knocking on doors for the nuclear freeze in 1984 and 1985.

So then the question would be, why am I now kind of a full-time political activist and analyst-polemicist and so on. The answer is that 9/11 outraged me to the point that I couldn't remain silent and focus on other things any longer. I learned that 9/11 was a blatant inside job dealing with the demolition of the World Trade Centre and the fake jetliner hit on the Pentagon in late 2003.

When I became aware of that I realized that pursuing my academic career as it then existed would not allow me to talk about those issues. I just finished my PhD and I would have to spend about ten years working on getting tenure and that would take me out of the game at the point when it was most important to be talking about this.

I started doing teach-ins, getting active with scholars for 9/11 truth promoting David Ray Griffin. I got him on C- SPAN, the first nationally televised talk on the 9/11 truth. Then that became a full-time occupation when apparently the Republican Party in the United States decided to use me as a kind of a whipping boy to scare the other professors away from looking at this issue. So they had their political hacks in the Wisconsin state legislature, led by Steven Mass, witch-hunted me and dragged me through the media in a very unflattering light, in an attempt to slow down the rise of the 9/11 truth movement in the academy. So this ruined my possibilities as an orthodox academician in the United States and forced me to take up alternative media and activism full time.

So I can't really claim credit for being so brave and principled that I would have chosen this for myself. It was thrust upon me, and so I just kind of took up the challenge that I found in front of me. Once I'd been witch-hunted in 2006, I suppose there was a point when the provost of the University of Wisconsin was begging me to go hide out and just not talk to the media. Had I done that, I have no idea whether I would still be employable in the academy. But I wasn't going to do that, because – as I told the provost, Patrick Farrell – I have been working to get this information into the public light for many years. Now that I was having some success in getting it into the public light, I certainly wasn't going to run away and hide.

So yes, at that point I suppose I could have tried to chicken out, but even then, I don't know whether if the scandal would have been a little bit smaller than it was. I still might not have been employable afterwards. So who knows, in Islam we sometimes say that when a law makes an opening for you, you need to take it. Allah definitely made an opening here.

How do you see the world today in terms of the challenges facing us?

Kevin Barrett

The world is obviously in a crisis. There are many dimensions to this crisis. There's the ecological crisis, there's a spiritual crisis in which spiritual knowledge has been obscured, and there's of course a humanitarian crisis as well. There's just a vast amount of unnecessary human suffering, and I think the solution to all of these crises would be kind of an interlinked change, that is, that solving one will solve them all. They're not really separate.

I think that a key issue is a kind of a transformation of consciousness, in which more ordinary people rise to a state of consciousness, more like that of the great saints and mystics of the past. I personally think that Islam may hold part of the answer for this, because in Islam everyone has to work on their spiritual state.

In Christianity and many other religions – including eastern religions – spiritual specialists are the ones who go out and fast and pray and work very hard in their spirituality. The ordinary householder is allowed to just sort of be a householder. In Islam there's no such thing as an ordinary householder nor is there such a thing as a monk. Every single Muslim has to do an arduous fast during the month of Ramadan. Every single Muslim is supposed to pray and go into a state of absolute submission to the absolute, five times per day. No Muslim is allowed to pile up wealth. Take that, Saudi Arabia. Charity is obligatory for Muslims.

If you're actually following Islam, you're following a path like that of the spiritual specialists – in the other religions – the priest, the mystics, and the monks. Every single Muslim is supposed to be that way.

Now of course in reality, there are plenty of Muslims who don't do very well at these things, but still the idea of a religion that insists that everyone raise their spirituality, I think is absolutely crucial.

I'm not saying that there aren't people who can't reach higher spiritual states through another path, and Islam recognizes that. It's the one Middle Eastern monotheism that is not trying to make everybody exactly the same.

But in any case I think that the average, the overall level of consciousness, the dominant tone of consciousness needs to rise considerably and that I think could happen partly through religious commitments, through people waking up and recognizing that material pursuits are not satisfying. Ultimately they are frustrating. We're all chasing carrots and dodging sticks and that process gets old very quickly. If you're given bigger and sweeter carrots, you just get used to them. So it doesn't help you, comfort doesn't help you.

If you use air conditioning, it feels great for a while, but then you just get used to that nice regulated temperature, and then a few degrees above that feel really hot. Whereas if you do what the Native Americans here in Wisconsin USA did and live without any air conditioning and with just a fire in a tent in the winter for heat, then you adjust to that. So this pursuit of material gratification and comfort – as wonderful as it feels when you get out of that heat into the air conditioning or out of the freezing cold into the heated space – it feels great for a while, and then you just get used to it. Basically, the pursuit of material comfort and pleasure doesn't get you anywhere.

There's a receding horizon and this is true at every level for every kind of material pursuit and pleasure. The only thing that actually gets you anywhere is an expansion of consciousness. As people realize this – that the kinds of incentives that drive people to fight with each other for power and pleasure in material pursuits will diminish naturally – that's what needs to happen, that's the basis of everything.

Politically, I think that political action that addresses that issue is the important kind... political action that just assumes the material universe with human nature at its most base level... such as orthodox communism, marxism, socialism, all forms of progressive Western currents of thought, are actually dead ends. Because they all take for granted this material space-time kind of paradigm, they take for granted that people are really just sort of mechanistic physical bodies with certain kinds of instincts.

Then with that as the paradigm you can't get anywhere. So we need paradigm-shifting political work. The only political work that matters is the political work that radically overturns paradigms and alters consciousness... shocks people out of their current state of consciousness.

This is why I think the red pill issues, the really huge emotionally charged issues like 9/11 truth, the assassinations of the Kennedys, Martin Luther King, Malcolm X, Paul Wellstone, the fact that we're ruled by vicious psychopaths – the fact that these vicious psychopaths routinely abduct and sexually torture and murder children as part of their Satanic religious rituals – these sorts of things are very shocking and that's one reason a lot of people avoid them. The orthodox-left people avoid these issues, because they can't handle the emotions and they imagine that people will never be able to handle their emotions, and so they're working in that paradigm of trying to readjust social reality within the material paradigm. That's doomed: it is not going to get us anywhere.

Instead, we need these red-pill issues that shock people awake, that turn their consciousness inside out, that allow them to step aside from ordinary consciousness they developed in this decadent civilization and taste something bigger and better.

Does it matter if we vote or not?

That's a very good question. I think that the best way to look at voting in elections is that they're another tool of power. We shouldn't imagine that the world in general and so-called Western democracies in particular are actually ruled by the people by way of elections and representative democracy. They're not.

They're ruled by oligarchs, they're ruled by mind-control specialists, and they're ruled by thugs, psychopaths, and military brutes – its sheer power using mass murder and big lies, that's how the world is actually run.

But elections and voting are one tool of power – a small one to be sure – but a real one. So I think that those who want to change the world should use that tool and every other tool that is available.

In my own case, I ran for Congress in 2008 here in the USA, not because I had any interest in winning or being anointed a representative and being sent to Washington, imagining that I would be actually ruling society through making the laws. That's a complete joke. I know very well that Congress does not rule America, by any means. The oligarchs with the money to buy and sell Congress people are the people who actually rule.

So when I ran for Congress I was using it as a tool of power to get the message out. I was able to get all sorts of interviews with mainstream media that I wouldn't have otherwise, and that was the reason I ran, not because I was interested in participating in the illusion that elected representatives actually govern, because of course they don't. That doesn't mean that people should ignore this particular tool of power.

I think it is again, as I said, everybody has different abilities and interests. Some people may change the world through producing art, others through being social media activists – there are an awful lot of those – and then some may be drawn to the electoral arena. So I think that's all good, and therefore the people who are interested in voting, running for office, certainly should do those things.

What are your thoughts about money and the global banks?

I think that the biggest scam in history is the counterfeiting of our currency by the international banksters, who produce most of the currency used in this world by lending it into existence and interest. It's backed by nothing. It's unimaginable, the depths of depravity, and the amount of money and power that this is producing, and this is really the central mechanism of power in today's world: counterfeiting of money by the banksters, and our entire money supply essentially is counterfeit.

So if we're going to change the way things work in terms of the power structure of the world, this is one of the first things we need to change, one of the basic targets that we need to have.

Kevin Barrett

There's no point in running for Congress, for example, and imagining you're going to make the laws, when the people really ruling the world are these international banksters: counterfeiters. If you're going to run for Congress, you need to be doing so in a way to wake people up and incite them to overthrow the international banks and counterfeiters.

Likewise with other kinds of actions, I think this is very central to every form of political reform that we can even imagine that would improve anything in the world today, which is we need to end this currency system and institute a transparent system that benefits ordinary people rather than this plutocratic elite.

What do you think about the debt-based economy people are stuck in, and is there a way out?

I think individuals can try to reorganize their lives to avoid debt as much as possible, but we're all stuck using debt-based money for many things. It's very difficult to avoid doing so, but I do think that we should try to organize our own economic lives to minimize our participation in this usury system.

That can be done in many ways, there's a sort of hierarchy of good and bad here in terms of how we use money. We should try to use less so-called credit from the banks and more cash.

And if possible we should try to use less cash and more alternative currencies, whether Bitcoin, or local currencies, or precious metals, or whatever alternative currency that we could possibly come up with.

We should be avoiding the big banks as much as possible to the extent that we have to put any currency or money – ordinary money – into banks. It should be a local credit union, not big banks. I think we should be riling people up and doing a lot of agitprop, polemical work on this issue, because this is an issue that people can relate to.

In 2008 when I ran for Congress, people were virtually unanimous – as all the polls showed – in opposing the banks' bailout, and yet the politicians voted for it and then enacted it against the wishes – the unanimous wishes – essentially, of their constituencies.

So people are on one side of this issue with no air and the banks are on the other side. The occupy movement also got this right and essentially operated under the motto: It's the banks, stupid!

I think that should be our motto in general. But I think this is a very good issue to focus on, and in some ways it's easier to get traction on this currency reform issue than other red-pill issues, like men learning the truth of assassinations which are scarier, but we need to work at it at every level, both in our personal lives and in the public arena.

We have started to read and hear about microchipping people. What does that mean?

Well, here in Wisconsin USA former Governor Tommy Thompson, who was the Director of Health and Human Services under George W. Bush and 9/11, has gone to work for a microchip company. He's gotten himself microchipped, and he has urged everyone else to get microchipped as well.

This is just one example of the trend that we're seeing. There are certain interests that would like to have everyone microchipped. This would be a kind of a fool proof identification tag. It would operate a lot like the mark of the beast, described in the Book of Revelations, a mark that people would have to have on their foreheads, on their arms, or their hands in order to buy and sell. It would be the ultimate social-control tool.

Ultimately, these microchips could be inserted in people's brains and deprive people of free will, turn them into human robots acting at the behest of whoever was controlling the system. So this is, of course, a nightmare dystopian scenario, and the problem is that so often people won't accept such things. Today most people would not rush down to get microchipped as much as Tommy Thompson urges them to. So ordinary folks aren't on board with the dystopian scenario. So those pushing it sensibly try to bring it in gradually.

There's the famous image of the frog being slowly boiled in the pot as [they] gradually raise the temperature of the burner and the frog doesn't jump out, because it never really feels the change. That's what's been going on in many different areas in terms of the transition to a dystopian society.

So they may start out by microchipping a small number of people in certain kinds of situations and then certain employers will require it. And they'll say: "Well, the government isn't forcing everyone to get microchipped, it's just these employers," and so on. Then there'll be a big fake terrorist attack, and then they'll say, "Well, we're going have to expand these microchips to all the suspicious people, all the immigrants." They'll bring it in gradually, and then before you know it, suddenly, everybody's microchipped and robotized.

So we need to resist this at the very beginning, just like everything else, it's important not to get started down the slippery slope towards dystopia, we need to resist REAL ID. We really should be working to eliminate all forms of positive identification. Society worked fine in the nineteenth century before there was any real identification that worked, even better in a lot of respects before that.

We need to transition to a society based on trust, based on spirituality, based on consciousness of moral ethical purity. There's no point in living in a society where we can't trust each other unless we're all microchipped and controlled by the government. That would be worse than humans just giving it up and letting other species take over.

So we really have to resist these things. They're creating a situation. These solutions are vastly worse than whatever the problems were that they're solving. And this trend towards an ultimately microchip society – which is in fact what Aaron Russo was told by Nick Rockefeller – is coming. Nick Rockefeller said before 9/11 that 9/11 was coming. "We're going to have an event," he said, and that the ultimate end game of this was going to be a completely microchipped and controlled society. And when Aaron Russo protested, Nick Rockefeller got angry and said, "Well, let's just take care of your family, your kids."

When Aaron Russo then – later after 9/11 – went public with Nick Rockefeller's foreknowledge of 9/11, and statements about getting towards a microchipped society. Aaron Russo was then given a fast-acting cancer, and died not long after that.

So these are the kind of psychopaths that we're dealing with, and they just have to be resisted it at every possible level.

What are your thoughts about depopulation?

Well, there's a discussion among people who are opposed to the New World Order about whether there may be a plan to massacre the majority population in order to get to a population level that the oligarchs would consider sustainable. It's unclear whether they mean sustainable in terms of the environment and the ecosystem, or sustainable in terms of their own control over humanity. There's no absolutely clear evidence and smoking gun that proves that any organised cabal is working towards this.

But there are a lot of indications and bits of circumstantial evidence that get cited, ranging from quotes from people like Prince Philip – or one of the British royalty – I think said he would like to be reincarnated as a virus that would kill off most of humanity in order to save the Earth. It's as a college freak myself that I can sort of relate to that. The eye of the problem is that I would never do it – even if I had the means to, which obviously I don't – whereas someone like a British royal family member and his oligarchical contacts might actually be in a position to create such a virus in a laboratory. So I think we do have to be cautious about such things.

There have been a lot of unexplained deaths of microbiologists, genetic engineering experts and so on... there is a lot of work being done, biological warfare around the world. There's a story that in the Republic of Georgia there are US oligarchy-related biological warfare labs doing totally illegal work.

Here in the United States we had the anthrax attacks launched by US, by our insiders designed to smear Muslims. These American germ-warfare people sent envelopes that read, "Death to America, Death, Death to Israel, Allah is great," falsely implicating Muslims in these attacks and contributing to the massacre of four million Muslims around the world, which followed the 9/11 anthrax operation.

So there're biological warfare experts doing terrible things around the world and there are certain members of the oligarchies on record saying they would much prefer a lower level of population. There are of course the mysterious Georgia Guidestones saying that population must be maintained at something like half a billion or something like that. We're seven billion now, so this would be a fourteen-fold reduction in human population. The only way to accomplish that rapidly would be through the biggest massacre in history by far.

We think we have to be concerned about the possibility that certain members of the elite might be doing this, and as genetic technology moves ahead it will become easier and easier for smaller and less organized and funded groups to massacre people, if they choose to do so. I think it was Frank Herbert, science fiction writer, who was quoted as saying many, many years ago, that it will soon be easy for any high school biology student to kill most of the world's population if he wanted to. Let's hope that's an exaggeration.

In any case though, we are on a trajectory towards trouble on the bio warfare front, without even getting into the issue of nation states using these techniques in their power struggles with other nation's states.

The Israelis are on record as having worked on genetic-specific or ethnic-specific bioweapons with South Africa, prior to the fall of apartheid, and certainly they've continued those efforts since. And undoubtedly, there are other groups doing this as well.

So this is all a very worrisome area, and one of the reasons that we need a total transformation of consciousness and the total transformation of a way of doing things is that if we just continue with business as usual in this particular area, we're almost certainly going to see horrific epidemics and die-offs, one way or another.

What is your opinion on vaccines, and is vaccination part of the depopulation question?

Well, there's a lively debate among the editorial staff of Veterans Today, where I'm editor, about vaccines. Gordon Duff, the senior editor, is married to a woman – she is a very nice woman – I've met them and I've stayed at their house – and she is a public health nurse and a teacher of Public Health. She's convinced that vaccines are basically a good thing. There is some evidence that some kinds of vaccines have had positive public health benefits. But there are also a fair bit of evidence that these benefits have not been nearly as massive as has been claimed, and that the downside and risks of vaccines are much greater than has been claimed. This would make sense just by looking at who's profiting, what interest groups are manufacturing the discourse for what purposes.

Clearly, the vaccine manufacturers, the pharmaceutical industry, the government people working in this domain all have a huge incentive to exaggerate the benefits and to minimize the risks in the drawbacks. So I think a fair-minded look at this issue would suggest that we need to be very cautious about vaccination.

Lynn Margulis– possibly the greatest biological scientist of the twentieth century, who passed away a few years ago after publicly questioning the 9/11 inside job – said on my radio show that the skin barrier is there for a reason. It is not a good idea to penetrate the skin barrier with hypodermic needles in order to put something straight in the bloodstream, because this just doesn't happen in nature. It's a totally unnatural thing.

So that's one aspect of vaccines that need to be questioned – the hypodermic route into the bloodstream – that's especially when you consider that the vaccinations are including all sorts of toxic material things, like formaldehyde and mercury, for example – putting that straight into the blood stream. Obviously this is a very, very bad idea.

It should only be done in the gravest emergency and when the evidence is utterly overwhelming that in that particular case that individual desperately needs that particular shot. There are, of course, other routes for vaccination: the oral route, which is much, much safer, much more preferable, if one needs a vaccine in the first place.

So in any case I personally come to the conclusion that the risk benefit equation is so unbalanced towards risk and towards damage that I made sure that my children were not vaccinated. They took a religious exemption after making a terrible mistake by allowing my first child to be vaccinated and dealing with the autism spectrum disorder that obviously resulted from that.

There was a huge trauma following the one vaccination we gave one of our children, and that was clearly related, and clearly, this is what obviously produced the autism-spectrum issue that afflicted him, and so many people have had exactly the same experience. So my advice would be that everyone should claim exemption from vaccines at this point, until a more sensible approach to vaccines is developed, one that is more balanced in recognizing the risks and drawbacks as opposed to the benefits.

What are GMOs?

GMOs are another symptom of this technocratic meddling with the world, this playing God that has become such a threatening characteristic of modern Western civilization. The GMO Frankenfood now are being produced in great quantities, especially here in the USA, thanks to big corporations like Monsanto that find this more profitable than other approaches and of course there are all sorts of indications that this genetic modification process is creating all sorts of problems.

We've had all the evidence that, for example, when they genetically engineer corn and soybeans to produce their own sort of insecticide, then the people... when you eat the corn and soybeans... or the animals that eat it... are getting the insecticide that's being produced biologically... well, it's still an insecticide, and likewise, there are so many cases like this where there are questions about the safety of GMOs, and more and more countries are banning them. I strongly support this anti-GMO movement.

Here in the US we have to work very hard just to get them labelled or even to pass laws allowing non-GMO products to be labelled as such.

This shows the overwhelming power of the pro-GMO forces, the big corporations that are profiting off this. I think they're ultimately trying to engineer a sort of brave new world in which this tiny elite – this oligarchy – has all the levers of power. By creating crops designed to work to thrive in the toxic environment that they're creating, it's ultimately going to put independent people out of business. All farmers will be dependent on these GMOs and the seed companies like Monsanto that are using them, and we'll have a totally unnatural world.

I think long before we reach that point, the whole thing will collapse. In any case, we're obviously on a path towards dystopia or oblivion. To get off it, I think we really should stop GMOs. I would call for a moratorium on all biological research in the genetic modification field. I think all research on the genome and all action, all modification of the genome, should be classified as a capital crime.

Let's just say if you have life imprisonment crime, all of the scientists who are doing this are essentially at war with humanity. I think we need to recognize that this is a war, and we need to fight back and put them out of business. They are ultimately trying to kill humanity, and they basically admit this, admit that within 30-50 years, if things keep going the way they are, we'll hit what they call a singularity, which will be a transition between the world that we're in now, with humans and animals and the natural ecosystem. We will move into a new world in which some form of synthetic life – whether it's been biologically or genetically engineered together with nanotechnology and artificial intelligence – that will take over. It's possible to create such so-called creatures that will use energy more efficiently than biological life does. So this stuff will just basically devour biological life and it'll be a cancer on the universe if that happens.

So those of us who want to defend humanity, the ecosystem, the animals and plants around us in our beautiful planet and biological life in general, we need to recognize that we're in a war to the death against these forces that are trying to exterminate us, to destroy biological life, and to create a cancer of artificial life that will threaten the entire universe. It is a cancer. It is a contagious disease that would move off from earth and destroy the rest of the universe. We need to stop this disease, we need to realize that it's both a war in which this enemy, the ultimate enemy, the ultimate cancer on the universe, needs to be exterminated, and it's also a disease that needs to be wiped out.

It sounds like an extreme position, but it's reality. I think the information component of this war is the most important one. But we should recognize that it would be worth any sacrifice that we could make to stop this process from threatening not only our own planet but the entire universe.

Do chemtrails exist, and if so, how would you describe them?

It seems fairly clear – I guess that's not the right metaphor. Seems clear as a clear blue sky. When we look up today, we don't see a clear blue sky very often. We are more likely to see these persistent chemtrails muddying up the sky, turning it into a sort of shade of off-white, with these very strange looking artificial clouds forming around these persistent chemtrails.

Many people believe that this is part of a secret program in which – among other things – aluminium, barium, and strontium are being sprayed into the atmosphere. Hypothesis would be that this is being done primarily to stop global warming. Supposedly, this is a kind of an atmospheric sunscreen being applied to save the planet from global warming.

I did speak to an investigative reporter, who is not really a truther, by the way. I met this guy in 2006, shortly before the big 9/11 truth conference in Chicago. He's an Indiana-based mainstream journalist who investigated the chemtrails issue. I don't think he ever published it, though. He said that he had had it confirmed that there are two separate chemtrails programs going on in the United States. One of them is producing a planetary sunscreen designed to slow or stop global warming. The other is altering the atmosphere by adding particles that will be useful in military imaging systems, radar-style imaging systems.

I suspect that he's probably right that these are happening. There are plenty of patents that have been taken out on systems for providing a global sunscreen to stop global warming. There are geoengineering conferences, there are folks out there telling us what geoengineering is, since it's real and admitted. Since there are geoengineering conferences, geoengineering patents, there's a whole expanding field called geoengineering. This is what we should be talking about.

Chemtrails has a kind of a dubious reputation these days, and there are those who deny that such things even exist.

But nobody can deny that geoengineering exists as an expanding field. So clearly, geoengineering is real if you're to say at the very least, they're doing experimental spraying of heavy metals and other things into the atmosphere. And it's possible that a major program aimed at impacting the climate is already going on.

This is in so many other areas – the first thing we need is total transparency. It's just – you know – even if this is being done with the best intentions, it's just utterly wrong that the public isn't being accurately informed about this, and about everything else.

So I think that we really need to have an all-out struggle for transparency. The people of the world need to rise up and say we're not going to take it anymore. We're not going to accept the situation in which our elites are doing all of these things in secret, even if they're for our own good, as the elites will say they are, we want to know the details, and we just can't accept the kind of a situation in which we don't understand. We don't have access to accurate information about what is being sprayed into the atmosphere and why.

Please share your thoughts about the environment and the current weather conditions.

Kevin Barrett

I honestly think that there probably is a carbon-based global warming problem. Many people in the alternative information community think it's a hoax, because they've seen so many similar situations in which a huge threat is manufactured by the oligarchy in order to stampede the herd of sheep in whichever direction the oligarchy wishes.

In this case however, I think the oligarchy may be dealing with a genuinely scary issue, which is that the carbon content of the atmosphere does seem to be closely related to the average global temperature. Now whether this is cause or effect – which is one issue that gets raised – it doesn't really matter, because if, as some people suggest, it's actually solar fluctuations that are driving global temperature changes, and that the carbon increases in the atmosphere a little bit after the sun starts heating up the planet, it's still the carbon that's doing most of the warming, because it's a feedback loop.

So even if it was the solar fluctuation that launches each period of global warming, and the carbon then comes later, it is the feedback loop in which the carbon plays a big role that's doing the actual warming.

Today, of course, we know that it's not even the carbon itself that does most of the warming, it's the water vapour. So there's a feedback loop in whatever the ultimate cause is. Even if it was the sun historically, it's actually the carbon increases in the atmosphere, and that leads to a little bit of warming which then evaporates water from the oceans, and that puts more water vapour in the atmosphere, and that water vapour is what does the majority of the actual warming.

Today humans are putting vast amounts of carbon in the atmosphere that is going to – even whatever the sun does – this is going to lead to relative warming compared to what would have happened otherwise. As the carbon raises the temperature, that raised temperature leads to the vapourisation of water from the oceans, and that water does most of the job of making the planet warmer.

So I would argue that on this particular issue the mainstream scientific consensus is not as wrong, as some people think. I think we do have a likely planetary emergency in this area. So I would guess that, in fact, this whole issue is very real.

There may be other issues that are equally urgent: radiation – the Fukushima disaster some say is looking like an extinction-level event. The oceans are toxic and becoming more acidic. Life in the oceans is dying off, even aside from the overfishing. So there are a whole lot of interrelated issues here and ultimately, I think that we are going to change our way of life and stop robbing our ecosystem, and putting our waste products out in such huge amounts that it makes our environment toxic.

Many other species have this issue where they increase in population to a level where their toxic effluents make their environment unsustainable and then they have a population crash.

There's no reason to believe that humans are on a different path. Sure we do have intelligence. We have a spiritual dimension. Theoretically, we should be able to deal with this, but we're still doing what all sorts of other species going down to sub-microscopic bacteria do, which is increased to the point that they excrete so many toxic waste products that they die off.

Whether or not you want to believe that these elitists are right that Earth's population is being knocked down to half a billion people. Of course, they're willing to do that by the most ruthless and horrific ways. I think you have to admit that we do have this kind of ecological crisis, and I think carbon-based global warming is part of the problem.

Do you have a practice that keeps your spirits high?

I guess you're referring to a spiritual religious practice, and yes, I do: the five times daily Allah prayer, prescribed in a group, which consists of a series of yogic postures culminating in this posture of absolute submission to the Absolute with your forehead on the floor. This is a time-honoured practice, of course, in the world of Islam. It's in fact a requirement for all Muslims – not that every Muslim perfectly follows it – but theoretically all one point five billion of us are supposed to do this five times every day – or some would say, three times every day, because you can collapse a couple of them together – Shia friends tell me that. Anyway, that practice I think is very, very helpful.

There are even people who are non-Muslims who have tried this salat prayer ritual and found that it's very beneficial in many ways. It's a kind of a meditation and in that moment of absolute submission with the forehead on the floor is a moment of deep meditation. So there's a kind of an ebb and flow that happens in that salat prayer that is unlike anything any other kind of meditative or spiritual practice.

I also do other forms of meditation. I learned how to do a kind of a Sufi meditation that consists of chanting various Koranic formulas when I was in Morocco. So I do that periodically as well. Then I sometimes do that without actual chanting, simply by focusing on the formulas, visualizing them, sort of imagining them, rather than actually chanting them.

There are many other forms of meditation – in other traditions that are quite similar – that employ chanting and sounds. I listen to the Koran which is another form of meditation, and there are some studies ostensibly showing huge spiritual benefits or even health benefits when people, whether or not they're Muslims, listen to the Koran – double-blind studies in which half the people listen to actual Koran, others listen to a Koran-like chanting in Arabic, but it's not the Koran. The people who hear the actual Koran end up much healthier.

So I'm following these traditional spiritual practices prescribed by Islam, and a lot of folks, including the Traditionalist – which is the dominant school in religious studies – argue that these Islamic practices have been better preserved than most other of the great traditions. This is one reason why people like René Guenon, the founder of Traditionalism, came to Islam. Even though he argued that all great traditions are authentic, he claimed – and many others have observed – that the Islam has preserved the actual chain of transmission back to the revelation, better than the other traditions have. I agree with that – it's one of the reasons that I did come to Islam and practise it.

So I respect the spiritual practices of other people as well. I used to practice Zen meditation and recognize that it works as well. It has its own benefits. Being an undisciplined sort though, for me the discipline of this required obligatory five-times-daily prayer in Islam is very helpful to me. It forces me to do this and make it a regular part of my life. And being sort of lazy and scattered, I'm not sure if I would be able to sustain a spiritual practice in some other tradition.

Seeing the madness around me, I feel hopeless. Can you suggest some ways that would help me regain my trust in the future, and how to act to make a positive change?

Well, I think I have a hard time imagining how one could have a kind of a materialistic world view – the consensus elite worldview in the West – and not be in just utter and total despair at every level. This dominant Western materialistic world would tell us that everything around us is just sheer accident without any kind of meaning, that we're condemned to losing what little benefit we're getting from this material world, which would be the power and pleasure, the physical pleasures, things like that, we're going to lose that as we get older, our bodies decline, and finally we die, and then lose everything we had.

This worldview that would tell us that that's really all there is, I think is deeply unsatisfying. And I really wonder how anyone could live a satisfying responsible life while adhering to that worldview. I think the basis of coming to both a more accurate and also a more life-affirming and sustainable kind of worldview is recognizing that the basis of reality is not matter, space, and time, but rather the basis of reality is consciousness, that the universe is much more like a dream than like a solid place.

And we know that scientifically from experiments in the field of PSI. The dominant paradigm in the Western Academy refuses to even consider this evidence. It's got its head in the sand, but this evidence along with work in quantum physics and other fields shows very clearly that the universe is just possibility or probability waves, until consciousness turns those possibility or probability waves into reality.

So once we know that and we realize that we're living in a dream and whatever you want to call the ultimate dreamer. I would call the ultimate dreamer God or Allah.

But however you choose to describe this, you need to recognize that the purpose of life is not just to thrive in the material space-time continuum and steal energy from the life around us and to have power and pleasure and all of that.

The purpose of life is actually more kind of contemplation and a development of our consciousness through contemplation. Once we realize that then we realize even if this whole space-time material world that we're in were to get blown up, the Yellowstone volcano could go off and make life impossible, all sorts of things could happen, we could have a huge die off, but even if that were to happen, it really wouldn't be that important, because it's the consciousness of all the people who've lived that's important in this consciousness.

It's not tied into space-time, so it doesn't really matter whether the consciousness has appeared on a planet that only lasted for a little while in that form, even got blown up or whether a planet lasts for a zillion years and then petered out, really the real issue is the consciousness. So once we know that, then we realize the purpose of our lives is to face challenges and develop our consciousness. And we can do that whatever's going on in the world around us.

Many people have found that prison is the best possible environment for developing their consciousness – Malcolm X being a classic example. So the bad stuff going on around us – it's like the walls or bars of a prison – isn't something that should make us depressed. On the contrary, these challenges and the prison bars around us... and we're all living in metaphorical prison in the space-time continuum... this is actually a beneficial situation for us and for the people around us in terms of improving our consciousness and raising our consciousness.

So I think that is the basic realization – that we need to live happily and productively in the world that we're in

Kevin Barrett

If you could plant one seed in the mainstream mind, what would that be?

I think that we're seeing a new Copernican revolution. I guess that the seed I would plant would be this new Copernican revolution that suggests that the entire worldview that we've been conditioned to accept, ranging from the political worldview here in the US – we're the good guys in the West – the West is the good guy. The other, that used to be the communists, now it's the Muslims that is the evil enemy. When we turn that inside out through, for example, recognizing the truth about what happened on 9/11/2001. This produces a political Copernican revolution, as the Pogo cartoon put it, "We've met the enemy, and he is us." But this Copernican revolution has many other dimensions as well – the spiritual one that I mentioned.

Copernicus, of course, famously told us that the earth goes around the sun and not the other way around. And likewise we need ultimately this critical revolution I suggested earlier that is the material space-time reality goes around true reality, which is consciousness. That consciousness is not just this epiphenomenon of material reality, just brain cells firing that produces the illusion of consciousness, as materialists tell us. Rather that consciousness itself is the ultimate reality and that the material space-time world is just an epiphenomenon of consciousness. So that's the ultimate Copernican shift that we need.

But they're all tied together – it's all part of one big Copernican shift. And if I could plant the seed of turning everybody's worldview inside out through this kind of composite Copernican revolution, I guess then that's what I would do.

A mind that is stretched to a new experience can never go back to its old dimension.

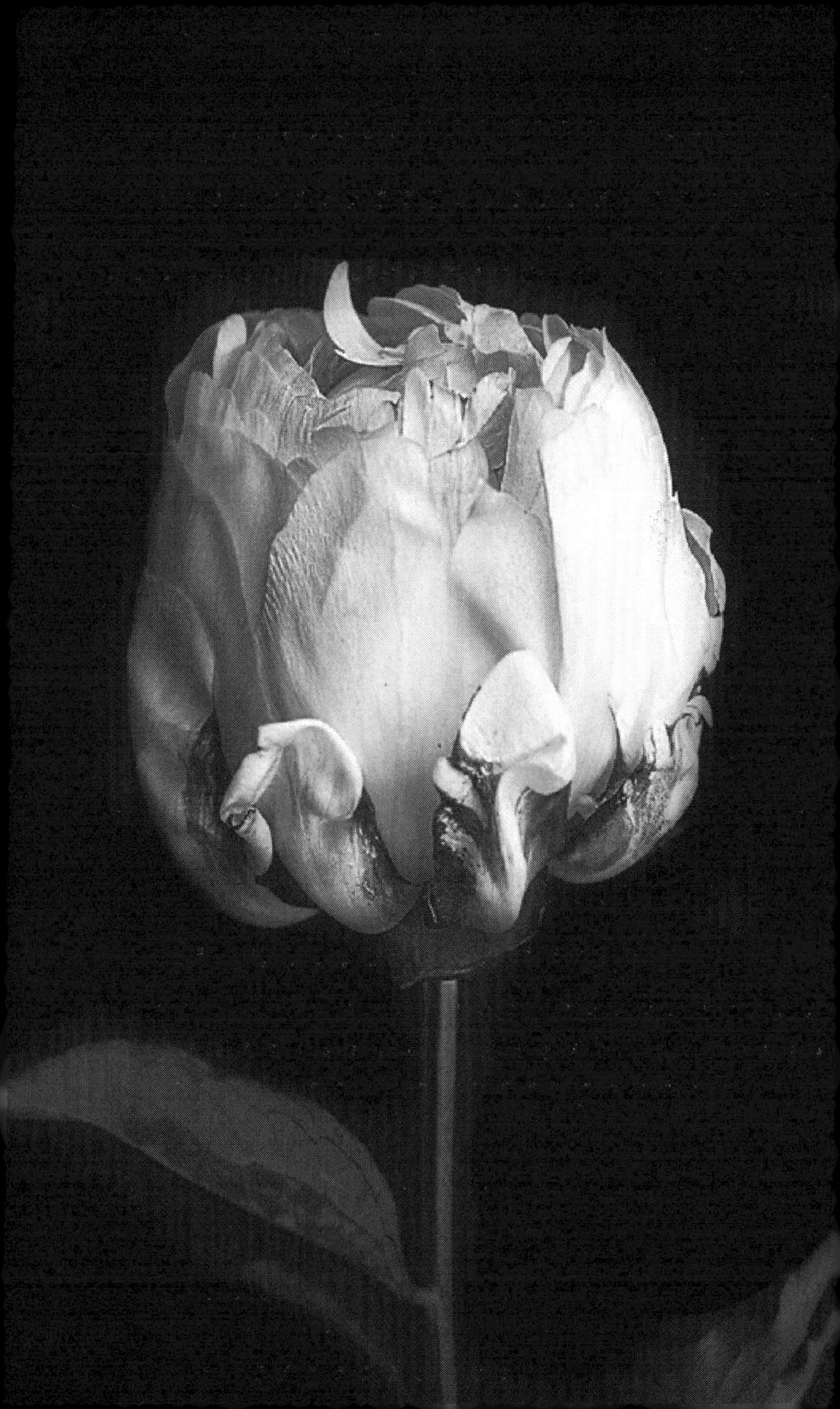

SOFIA SMALLSTORM

Sofia Smallstorm

SOFIA SMALLSTORM

Introduction

Sofia Smallstorm is known for the documentaries, *9/11 Mysteries* and *Unraveling Sandy Hook*. Sofia is also recognized for her research on the connections between geoengineering and synthetic biology.

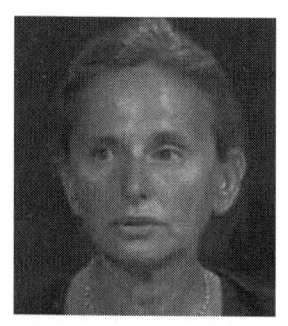

www.aboutthesky.com

When did you start exploring your field? Was there a specific event that led to this path of waking up.

Well, I don't even know that I have a field, other than sheer curiosity. So when did I become curious? You could say when I was a little girl. I would ask my mother, how do governments all get along? They are all governments, they're separated. They have their own countries, their armies, their oceans in between languages, there are different religions. How do they all get along?

And my mother just looked at me and she said, "Well, they all just work it out. They all just get along." Only today, much later in my time, no, no, they don't get along, they're all ordered along, because they have been whipped into line. They're controlled by loans and banks, superpowers. They are squirming, many of them. Countries are not comfortable in the hierarchy of the world. It's a very unjust, a very unprincipled hierarchic arrangement.

But my mother was having to deal with a five-year-old. One can't really explain much to a five-year-old, but I should have been given a pat on the back for my instinct that something may not be quite right. It's not a jigsaw puzzle that fits completely.

So that's when I really began to be curious. And I have the luxury, or privilege you could say, of living all over the world. My dad was in the diplomatic corps, and I went from the Third World, where I witnessed extreme poverty, like in India, to the civilized world, you could say, the western world.

After that I lived in Communist Europe. We could travel, of course, take holidays to Poland and Hungary, and so forth, so I saw countries in Communist Europe, and I could see that the drape of communism was heavy upon the people, and they cried so much.

I could see people with tears in their eyes, and I would ask my mother, "Why is everyone crying?" She would say, "It's the communists." I actually lived through the Communist – the Russian invasion – of Czechoslovakia. I was only a small child, and my mother – this was in the late sixties – my mother threw open the bedroom door one day and said, "Children, there is no school today. The Russians are here." We sleepily said, "The Russians? Okay." So we had to stay home. There were tanks rolling through the city and this was a military occupation I had never seen before.

So after that I lived in North Africa which was freshly independent. The country I lived in was Algeria. It was under the yoke of colonization until very recently. These were all rich countries – Libya, Algeria – and they were now allowed to develop with great oversight. There was tremendous presence of Americans' oil companies there, and American geologists were all over the place, advising the North Africans on how to drill for their oil.

Anyway, so that was a different culture. I was exposed to Muslim culture, Arabs, the Arab language. I learned how to speak French. After that I moved to Northern Europe, Scandinavia, Sweden.

There it was a whole other experience. Now this was very progressive compared to the Muslim, north-African country had lived in before. It was full of drugs, and kids were dropping out of school – blue jeans and long hair and carousing – and it was all very free. I was only a teenager, a young teenager, twelve, thirteen. I got to witness and experience liberalism in progress and freedom. But it was all socialist as well.

So there was tremendous regulation on people's lives. I wasn't a very old person, so I didn't really understand fully what I was living in. And I was a foreigner and that's the thing, I've always been a foreigner wherever I have lived – and felt like that. I still feel like that living in America.

So we went to France after that, and that was capitalist and very much like Northern Europe in some ways. But very rapid – it that was a rapid culture. The French do everything fast. They speak fast, they drive fast.

After that it was America itself, and this was considered that pinnacle of where you would want to live. Everybody wants to move to America from other countries, anyway because of business prospects. Anyone can become a millionaire in America. So the feel of opportunity, and even avarice – in that sense that you could make lots of money and become very rich.

That I felt the most in America, and I felt the most spiritual vacancy, the lack of spiritual deprivation in the way that the culture was put together. So the coolest people – when I got here as a mid-teenager – the coolest people were trying to achieve spiritual fulfilment. That was the beginning of the new age. That's just my take as a teenager.

How do you see the world today in the terms of the challenges facing us?

Well, that's a huge question. I see the world as becoming increasingly compressed in terms of its possibilities. It's almost like you're in a chamber, and the pressure is being increased and increased and increased. Then it's getting very difficult to breathe and move, and you're feeling that your life itself is becoming challenged, and you're going to have to think really creatively of a way to break out of this chamber.

So to me the answer to that is, we have to do something extraordinary within ourselves, something almost metaphysical, if not metaphysical.

We have to exert some capacity that is perhaps latent in us. We've got to start using that. We're in a heavy pressure situation, and it's only going to get heavier.

Does it matter if we vote or not?

I don't believe that voting achieves anything except the illusion in certain people's minds that they have expressed their desire. Because who gets up there to become elected? The processes by which votes are counted in controlled. All of that to me is very, very easily rigged. It's just lip service. Real votes are action in and how we live our lives.

Some people say you vote with your dollars. Where do you spend your money? But in some ways it's impossible. You cannot have electricity without paying the electric company. So there are certain dollars – given the confines – that how most of us live – that you've got to spend in certain places. We're not voting with our true choice-making ability. I don't want to say it's impossible to do that, but it's harder and harder to do that now.

What are you thoughts about money and the global banks?

That is an extremely artificial and extremely addictive and extremely manipulative situation. I just very recently came up with the idea, the mental image of a circus tent with poodles on their hind legs, wearing little skirts and having a little red hat, and we're all these poodles. We have convinced ourselves that we need this thing called money, which is now divorced from any real worth. It's not connected to gold – the fiat currency – it's not connected to anything, and it's just free-floating.

The people at the very top of our global structure make the money out of nothing as long as they've got us. Money is like our oxygen pipe – if you could picture a person in a hospital, hooked up to oxygen, sucking, sucking for life, that oxygen, that's what all of us are doing with money. We absolutely need more of it.

We don't understand that that's not what we need more of. We need more of our own internal wealth, our own power to create our own intuition, innovation. You can think up really creative ideas and solutions to your life any minute of the day.

I'm constantly inventing little ways to solve problems around my house that I don't have to get anyone else to do or pay anyone for. You can solve your problems very creatively – a lot of them – and if more people did that, more people did that together – but you have to start really small. You have to start with your best friend or your brother and sister.

So what do you think that about the debt-based economy people are stuck in, and is there a way out?

Well, that's part of the money system. There is a way out. It's all about interaction. You need someone else to interact with. You can live as a hermit. If you're going to pull roots and eat off the trees and berries and what remains in these dying forests around us. But ultimately we're social, and we want some companionship, whoever you interact with, whatever exchanges you make with those people. That's how you can get out of debt, but unfortunately, our society is so ultra-structured now that we can't easily come up with certain essentials that we need to survive.

One of the shortcomings of being human is we've got no fur. We don't hibernate for the winter like a bear going to sleep for the cold months. Constantly, this physical body is constantly prodding us and saying, "I'm cold, I need another sandwich, I need to sleep."

So in taking care of our physical needs we have been made to feel very, very vulnerable. And again when you look at the spectre of debt, we've been told now that our things can be resolved, our problems can be solved, if we turn to greater structures above us – the government, for instance, state agencies. We can rely on them for their "kindness" which might come in the form of a vaccination program to keep us from getting sick.

So there's a tremendous culture of myth and mythology and complete blatant falsehood that we've been wrapped in, and debt is just part of that.

We have started to read and hear about microchipping people. What does that mean?

Microchips to me are things that are inserted into the body for location purposes and possibly release of frequencies – anything you put into your body that's artificial and you keep it there. It's the beginning of marrying with a machine technology, marrying your biology with machine technology – to agree to having something in your body that somebody else has access to remotely, that informs them about you. Again, that's a conscious awareness that you have exercised.

The question to me is how many people really understand what they've now become a partner with? And do they truly believe it's for their safety? I think a lot of people are being fooled into thinking that this will enable them to be safer. But it's the marriage with the technological age on the biological level with your consent. This is another thing we have to consider: what are we consenting to? We're consenting all the time.

What are you thoughts about depopulation?

Some say we're in an age of another extinction. The fact is, if you look at the land mass of the earth, we're not really overpopulated.

We're just more concentrated. An example is that, by the year 2000, 80 percent of the American population was living within an hour of the coast. So we're becoming concentrated in cities. As they bankrupted the small farmers in the heartland of America, the big farms moved into Con Agra – huge, huge Monsanto farms. They mechanized farming. It became a corporate activity – a big business activity. The people, the small people, had to go elsewhere.

So there's been an influx into cities and suburbs and an effort of the people to remake their lives there. When you concentrate population by dislocating them first, you actually can access them more easily. You can start trend making and propagandizing and influencing the lives and thoughts of the people when they're clustered – more easily than you can when they're spread apart.

It's very possible that there is a depopulation agenda. If there were a direct depopulation agenda, then that would be very easy to accomplish, because the weaponry and all of that is quite accessible to those who might wish to diminish our numbers.

But I see this more as a selection agenda. There are great numbers of programs in effect now that are harmful to biological health, which doesn't just mean us, it means the plants and all the organisms on the planet, animals. There's going to be a keeling over of many species, many kinds of life, there is already. The whole nature of how we live on the planet is changing. We are being compromised physiologically, biologically at a rapid rate.

This is not a great observation of biology. How is population biology reacting?

So a number of us human beings are developing cancer at an increasing rate. And degeneration, degenerative conditions, Our systems are failing and closing down on us, our tissues are calcifying, and cells are dying. It's because of the challenges we're surrounded by.

But this is what is of interest. So depopulation is more of an observation process.

Who survives this, who can withstand the stresses and the challenges and manage to live through and be breathing at the end of it all, that will be a more hardy prototypical form. The post-human world humanity 2.0 will be modelled on that cold form.

What is your opinion of vaccines, and vaccination's part of the depopulation question?

It is part of the challenge platform. The introduction of foreign materials into the body, not being addressed first by the twofold immune system that we have. We have a TH1 gateway cell-mitigated portal immune system which includes our skin and digestive tract, all of which act as filters. They are like the sentries at the gate, they say, "What's coming in? Oh my, we can't have this!" You go through reflexive movements like blinking, sneezing, itching, vomiting, diarrhea. That's all part of the first stage in your immune system – the TH1 immune system.

Then if something gets into the bloodstream and it shouldn't be there – for instance, complex oils and proteins that are included in vaccine formulas – they know oils and protein shouldn't be coming through the skin. They can when you have an open wound, but they shouldn't be, otherwise. They should be digested and broken down, put into an acid pool, decomposed molecularly into different kinds of fats.

But when it comes directly into your blood by way of a needle, your second immune system – which is your TH2 system, the humoral immune system – it goes nuts, and it starts producing antibodies, and it says, "What, what? Oh my gosh, we've got to protect against this."

So that's the antibody manufacturing system and the over-production of antibodies. That's what has caused so many allergies in people, so much confusion of our immune system.

So anytime you allow things to be put in your body, that's your consent again, without understanding the ramifications thereof. It's going to be positively, extremely dangerous.

The fact that they're brainwashing us into thinking that vaccines are safe and effective, safe and effective – all they're doing is using two little keywords repetitively – safe and effective, safe and effective. Everybody nods along like sheep and poodles and says, "Yes, yes. I want those. They are going to keep me safe. They're effective."

So ultimately, they're going into a different system. If they're going to debunk their own vaccines – that is my prediction – they're going to go into something called IGT: immunoprophylaxis by gene transfer. They have already started the experiments with this in labs. They want our muscle cells to produce the antibodies, not the plasma cells, which is where antibodies are currently produced. So they want to bypass the bloodstream and where they do inject you. They will always argue and say, "We don't put vaccines into your blood. We put them into your muscle and from there they get absorbed into the bloodstream." So it's just a dodge on their part.

But when they enact this – if they're ever successful at it, in IGT prophylactics by gene transfer – your muscle cells are going to make the antibodies. And your blood isn't going to have anything to do with it. They say that they're going to put in genetically, created of compounds that will induce your muscle cell to produce antibodies to get this that or the other thing.

But once again you're consenting to invasion of a kind that you're not capable of understanding on the biological cellular level.

What are GMO's?

They're also genetically altered organisms that are put into crops, for instance, and gene spots – transferring, combining, and mixing genes from one species into another – genes get mixed: fish genes and tomatoes, and they cause a different result.

I don't know how long they've been playing with this, but they managed to create drought-resistant crops, aluminum-tolerant crops. They're trying to modify the natural world to respond to specific introductions to specific things that have never been the case naturally.

When they can do that, then they can select and breed the entire topography of the world and all of its species and all of its life forms as they wish.

Depending on the perspective you're coming from, if you are in science, and you're so compartmentalized and so absorbed and living this life, and you're being rewarded for your findings – you're being promoted and praised and thousands of people in related fields are looking up to you, then you're not thinking of your work as scary, or it's not good, or you're thinking it's fantastic, and if you are groomed from babyhood practically to believe that you're making a contribution – you're saving the world – and science is the answer and this technocracy – I just learned that word – we live in a technocracy now whereby there's been a marriage of technology and politics – you can say technology and the corporate world – and it has transcended and taken over the entire top structure of the world pyramid. So everything is technocratically governed now.

We've got technology marrying with politics. All the agendas have to do with science. They're all blending "science as savior of the planet" into their goals.

That's being translated through – a friend of mine taught me – campaigns, literal ad campaigns. They go on television that are full of people from all over the world, talking about how we need to save the planet.

This is UN-created propaganda and we're all being urged to unite as one people with the intention of living with as small a footprint as possible. And science is going to show us how to do that. It's going to show us how to save ourselves and solve all our problems.

Do chemtrails exists? If so, how would you describe them?

Well, our clouds have changed. It depends on what you define as a chemtrail. The popular term now is geoengineering, which is a bigger concept than chemtrails itself. A chemtrail refers to a streak in the sky that's left behind a plane that starts morphing and lingering far longer than it should, and that has the ability to spread and form haze. These trails happen in groups, so they will eventually white out the sky. But these aren't natural layers of haze or droplets.

So there is a new creation process going on above our head, whereby something is being dispersed in the atmosphere, and it binds with atmospheric moisture and creates what looks like super-fine droplets clustered into layers of clouds. All the natural clouds that we grew up with – the real cirrocumulus, cumulonimbus cirrus, and cirrostratus – the combinations – we don't see those anymore, they're gone. I very, very occasionally see real cirrocumulus clouds where I live, and in Southern California. They usually happen after there's an engineered storm on the sea and they blow in from the ocean.

But apart from that, the clouds are all streaky and suspicious looking. And yet you'll see people bring their folding chairs to the beach and their wine and they sit and watch the sunset through this collection of absolute crazy stuff that they think are beautiful clouds.

Please share your thoughts about the environment and the current weather conditions.

Well, the environment is also taxed beyond its ability to bear anything. One of the natural responses of the biological life is to adapt. So for instance, if the wind blows on a tree from the time it's a tiny shoot to growing into a bigger thing with a trunk and branches, and the wind is blowing, blowing, blowing always from one side, that tree would start to lean over. Eventually the tree may fall to the ground. It may get so top-heavy that it can't stay upright, and it'll uproot self. But it's effectively trying to deal with the conditions that it finds itself in.

If biology on the cellular level and the level of organs and systems can't get rid of something, can't address it effectively and create solutions in the bio terrain for whatever the challenge is, then it will eventually begin to adapt. It will try to integrate itself and its mechanism, and in that effort it may give up and the organism may die entirely or become diseased on a constant basis, and weaker as time goes by, or it may simply die. So that's really what's happening environmentally.

Everything is struggling with these many, many programs and many challenges, and we are attempting to adapt.

The body has an injury response when it provoked significantly. Cells and systems can jump into quick redress. They can respond with alacrity and better organization than normal, and you think that you're actually getting better – you're healing. But over time, your system is not going to be able to handle those provocations successfully. It's going to give in. So temporarily a lot of us are showing enough resistance. But most of us are not going to be able to put that show up for long. Then some of us who do adapt – however that's possible – it may happen over generations, where successive lineage will start, for instance, being able to tolerate radio frequencies because they've become so prevalent. But that's not happening now. Now, you're just getting the response from sick organisms who are getting symptoms and loss of fertility, and so forth.

But you may eventually get a radiation-tolerant type of human. This would be part of the selection process. The people who can manage to get through this with the organisms within, across all the species, that can manage to get through, this will definitely be the hardiest and the strongest, and will be the ones that will then be further developed for greater proliferation.

Do you have a practice that keeps your spirits high?

Apart from little routines certain things in your life which you know can always manage to do, like my hot tea in the morning and walks and just personal little routines and regiment those keep me sane, these are the building blocks of what keep you going.

Seeing the madness around me I feel hopeless. Can you suggest some ways that will help me regain my trust in the future and how to act to make positive change?

This is the challenge, Kim, of being alive today in the world where we are and when we are. There's something – whatever created, impelled or compelled us into being here alive on this planet in this time

– is in some ways behind us. You could turn to that, to that creative force that made you. You could say something like, "How can I be the best that I can be?" Then you would have to go find yourself or get guidance on some level.

But I don't know anyone well enough to give that kind of spiritual advice.

If you could plant one seed in the mainstream mind, what would that be?

I would say open your being and eyes and develop the courage to see what's really going on around you and you got to get informed. You got to start talking and sharing this with other people. Stop discussing nonsense. Which I actually think is a way that people are comforting themselves. They discuss nonsense because it's mild and it does not threaten anyone and it doesn't rock anyone's boat any further then it's already being rocked, internally, psychically and physiologically from simply just trying to grasp and process what the hell is going on.

Let your light shine so brightly that others can see their way out of the dark

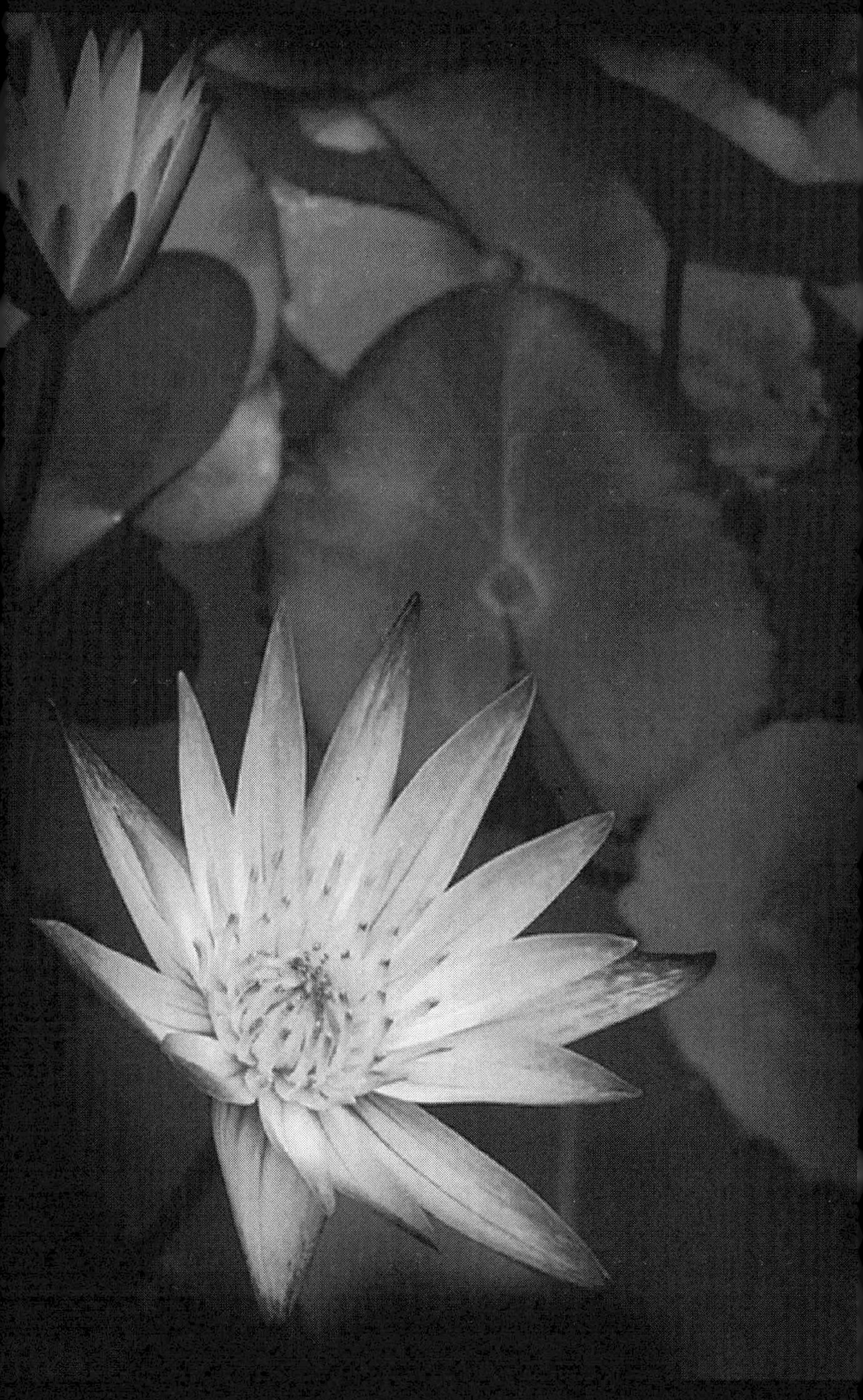

ZEN GARDNER

ZEN GARDNER

Introduction

Zen Gardner began his online writing and blogging 8 years ago after a lifelong quest for truth and several major life changes. His focus is empowering humanity to reach its full potential in conscious awareness and its resultant activation.

He writes on a variety of subjects from forbidden knowledge and our manipulated spiritual and historical context, to current political events, in an effort to dismantle old mind sets in order to encourage the awakening of human consciousness and bring meaningful change to a world that's under full frontal attack by powers that seek to deny humanity its health, freedom and ultimate discovery of who they truly are.

www.zengardner.com

When did you start exploring your field? Was there a specific event that led you to this path of waking up?

I went through several major life changes beginning when I was in college back in the late 60s and early 70s, when there was quite the upheaval happening in the United States and around the world amongst our generation.

I began to explore mysticism and philosophical questions. That was my major in university, but it didn't really ring true until I woke up to what was going on around me, and had various personal experiences. And I realized the most important thing in my life: it was to find out who I was and why I was here.

Until I could answer those questions, it didn't make much sense to go out and get a job like university was grooming me to do. Nor was anybody that I knew – who had those kinds of jobs – very happy, so that did not appeal to me.

So I decided to take off and travel the world for the next twenty or so years, which really opened my eyes, and I raised a young family overseas, and after that I eventually went back to the United States.

I went through a lot of changes all during that time: different philosophical modes, religious experiences. I went back to the States and then what woke me up the last time was just how manipulative society had become.

And then 9/11 being such a frightful event, I realized this was a time to really become active in the world. Because if it continued the way it was, it was not looking good for my kids, my grandkids, nor anybody else on the planet, so I wanted to become active.

So I pursued information furiously, and my eyes opened wider and wider and wider to the big picture, thanks to the Internet, I must say – the information explosion. That's when I started writing, started my blog, and became very active.

How do you see the world today in terms of the challenges facing us?

Wow, there's so many challenges coming at humanity from so many different directions. It's becoming more difficult to summarize them all the time between our deliberately toxified food, air, and water, the genetic modification of plants, animals, and even humans now... the alteration of our planet, the fracking and oil disasters many of which are manipulated. It's bringing out a real crisis from every direction.

And socially: what they call social engineering has been in play for hundreds of years, if not thousands, but more sophisticated in the last couple of hundred years to where education has become dumbed down. Our children are not given a chance to have an analytical mind to really understand the world the way it really is. But they're told what to think and what to do, and are being groomed for positions and subservient jobs without a chance... on top of other things they're doing to kids... with all the psychotropic drugs and the vaccines... and life has become a real battleground from so many different directions.

It's something that I've tried to address regularly in my writing and what I post on my website and people I network with and projects I'm involved with.

But information I think is key to all of this, so people can have a handle on realising just to what degree they are being literally attacked by some sort of coherent force that wants to subrogate humanity. It really is that drastic. Most people don't want to wake up to that reality, but that happens to be the way it is. At which point they'll become active, too. They'll realize that their own family, their own lives are at stake.

We are in a very serious situation. Never mind all the political and economic manipulations. These are all being done very, very arrogantly by money lenders who make profit off of lending money. That's all they do, they don't work. They just sit back and take money by lending money and then also giving conditions to that money... where people and countries are supposed to do – as a result of being loaned money – that they have to pay back, plus interest.

So it's a very serious thing. Never mind the media – there's another whole sector where people are being dumbed down – not just of the educational system, but by the mush that they're fed through the television sets, and now they've become addicted to it. So we have almost a comatose humanity. But I'm happy to report people are waking up. It's a very exciting time to be alive.

Does it matter if we vote or not?

I don't think so, except locally. I think our one place that we could make a difference is in very local government, where we can put responsible people in charge – people we actually know – and start from there. I don't have much faith in the way the structure is now, out of the whole political system, and the way it's dealt in.

I think it has to come down, and has to be redone completely. I believe in the early tribal societies where people there were the elders and respected wise people, who had pretty much the last say and helped direct.

But they were benign. They were loving and weren't trying to control or beat down their fellow tribesman, as opposed to what we're seeing today in humanity.

What are your thoughts about money and the global banks?

The whole money system – similar to what I just said about the political system – is completely wrong. I don't think that either can be reformed, if we had a real monetary system of exchange, which was based on real exchange, mostly goods for goods, and barter, and things like that.

But when there is a medium of exchange, if it was handled responsibly – from what I understand – most people would only have to hold some kind of a public job one or two days a week. And the rest of the time, people could be developing life and training their children and – you know – celebrating our existence here.

It would be nothing as we see it now. Unfortunately again, people look for this kind of affirmation of what we've got, whereas the fact is that we need a complete revolution, complete rethinking, redoing, which is why I write so much about becoming conscious before you start making any decisions.

Einstein famously said," We can't create a new world from the same level or solve today's problems, from the same level of consciousness that created them."

Unfortunately, most people are doing that. They're not waking up fully as to our true potential and the vast spiritual resources that we have – and they are operating according to old instructions – without even realizing it in most cases.

But I think that applies to the money system, and as I said, it applies to the political system, but we have very wicked people in control. They want power. They're not even happy with money. It is worse than greed. It's a very strange psychopathic characteristic in the so-called ruling classes that people take it for granted.

So again back to the elections. Locally, if people could just realize that your appointed so-called representative reports to you, that they are representing you... they're not some power figure that tells you what to do... but that's been reversed, where people are looking to authority just as they look to the media to tell them what's true and what's not true.

People are giving away their personal authority, giving away their own magnificent sovereignty to these imposed authorities. I think this is reflected in just about every area you look at.

What do you think about the debt-based economy in which people are stuck, and is there a way out?

Well, this makes me jump to a personal feeling I have. The world's economy is about to implode. It's living this so-called debt that isn't really there. That's the exchange currency. It's not even money anymore, it's just a computer – computer numbers that have no real value. If you try to change your money for like it used to be, based on gold or silver, you won't get that anymore, there's nothing behind it.

But this New World Government is trying to take its place via the UN and all these agencies and corporations and all, because they want to centralize control – which is the whole thing behind it – it's not for the good of humanity.

What they could easily do to solve these entire so-called crises which they themselves have engineered, is just to wipe all the debt clean and say, "Everybody's forgiven, but in exchange, we're going to give each of you a certain number of credits, and it's going to be in a little chip under your skin, or it's going be on a stamp on your body, and with this you can buy, you can sell, and everything will be forgiven."

All you have to do is take this thing, and everything will be cool, and everything will be integrated through a centralized computer system, and it'll all be fair, and everybody will be equal.

The only catch is: that is the ultimate in personal control.

If you do something out of step with what this New World Government structure has in mind, they'll just turn off your chip remotely, and you can't buy, or you can't do anything. So it's a very nasty plan, but they're going to bring it in – I think personally – one of the ways is through an economic plan that's going to look like forgiveness of debt and all that. And again, we're talking very serious centralized manipulative control.

But for people to wake up to that reality is a bit startling... but they're starting to see it: that people are losing their pensions, losing their homes, they're losing their savings, for no other reason than the so-called payback to the central banks, these other banks and other made-up reasons, so that people are starting to realize that they're losing things, that... "Wait a minute, this is not a level playing field we're on! Something's amiss!"

We have started to read and hear about microchipping people. What does that mean?

Well, there's an agenda called – well, a phenomenon – called transhumanism. That's a mixture of humans with machines, and it's being done on a massive scale. You can read about it on any science website: the latest – whether it's a robot or a bionic arm – they're bringing it in, like some kind of a medical miracle.

But now, as you can see in the news, whether it's Google Glass or any of these things, they actually have implants, not only pads – they put it on your head to affect and control and monitor your brain – but they can put them inside your body.

But if you look at what we're being shown in the movies today, they are all about that. If you look at Iron Man and these different movies where it looks like you can become super human by just having these super duper machines... so-called... to aid your body, and the really sad and frightening thing is how children, our younger generation, are falling for this, thinking this is wonderful, this is cool, it's hip.

And as you can see people are getting groomed into this dependence on technology. Just walk down the street: everybody staring at their telephone and not even talking to each other.

So technology: I think there's nothing wrong with it, inherently, but that it's to be used, not use you. That's where people ought to draw the line. But to implant it and integrate it into the human system is another form of control, where people would literally be induced into a state of loving their slavery... which is something George Orwell talked about in his book, 1984... the ultimate built-in control is to get people to love their slavery and their servitude. You can read about it in document after document back then: Aldous Huxley and the Societies of Orwell's.

But even before that, they talked about this: the ultimate control that people love being controlled. So it's something that people need to be aware of, and snap out of the trance.

What are your thoughts about depopulation?

I know it is a real agenda and it is something that the so-called elites have talked about for a couple of centuries. It was originally called eugenics, where they were to eliminate certain races or undesirable people from the population, because they weren't considered fit, that they are polluting the bloodlines of humanity or the genetic line... exposed to what they were going to, back to World War II.

But they're continuing on, people like Bill Gates... he openly talks about using vaccines to reduce the population by 15%. You can read quotes from very famous people talking about their issue of depopulation as a very important one.

When I was in college there was a book that came out called The Population Bomb, where they were programming our whole generation to just tell you there's too many people, there's too many people. So there is an agenda, and it is ongoing. That's what's happening with the geoengineering of chemtrails in our skies, the poisoning of our food and water: people's immune systems are getting worn down.

And now people can't reproduce, just from poisoning females from aspartame, from a lot of these chemicals, from the glycoside in the Monsanto Roundup herbicide. These all reduce fertility drastically, so that we are already decreasing in population from that side.

But as we know, as people are realizing, now that these bio labs that are making bio weapons around the world... I mean... who the heck would ever think we need such a thing... never mind how laboratories all over the world... so when these things... so-called "escape" accidentally – like this Ebola thing, if it's even real – it's no wonder that they're out there propagating these kinds of things, but these are all vectors again to come at humanity and to try to slow its growth, and people are very concerned it's going to be even more drastic measures.

I mean, as on ongoing plan, these people think long term. So if we can't reproduce and the population is declining and health is declining rapidly... . The world... you know, they're already marching towards this objective and it's a declared objective. There is a thing in the United States called the Georgia Guidestones. They were put up by some mysterious person. They say one of the top commandments of these stones – written in eight languages – says, to maintain humanity's population to five hundred million.

So that's a reduction of about 80-90 %. On top of all this, the world is not overpopulated. There's plenty of room – it's been proven scientifically that the whole world could live in Texas in the United States, just that one state and everybody would have a home. That's how drastically disproportionate this whole concept is over population. What they've done is they've herded people into population centres that are overcrowded, but they don't need to be. That's just the way the economy has been manipulated and they depend on living there for jobs.

Even now you'll see – through such programs as Agenda 21 and many of the UN programs – they're deliberately moving people off the land into population centres, and you'll see this in the news every day, especially in the United States. They go after people living out there on their own. So it's all part of the same program, but it's based on very fundamental lies, and overpopulation is one of them. It's a question of... if we shared our resources... there's plenty of food for everybody, if we stopped messing with people's economies, and the way they grow things. Well then, countries that normally... before they use that... farm all kinds of foods to feed their own populations.

Now the big corporations come in: all they farm is one product. They are dependent on importing from other countries. That was all set up, that is not a natural progression, by any means. Liberia, for example, only harvests rubber and the people there... they have to forage for other kinds of foods. It's not just rubber that is an example. Like in India they're doing soy and these are mega corporations that come in and buy off the land and the people feel helpless.

You probably heard that they've also been putting the GMO seeds out there. Over one hundred thousand Indian farmers have committed suicide, because they can't make a living and their families are suffering and it's a futile life for them, so this is drastic. But those are the kind of headlines you will not going to hear of in mainstream news.

What is your opinion on vaccines? And is vaccination part of the depopulation question?

Yes, definitely. Even Gandhi said that vaccines are one of the most dangerous things you could get involved with... this immunization, and then there may be a place for a certain kind of immunization, but most of it takes place naturally. Kids used to play outside. They played in the dirt. Your body would develop antibodies naturally by living a more natural life. Now plus too, a lot of diseases are engineered. What they've done is they re-released some of these. Smallpox was stamped out, but they kept it in laboratories. Now it's been re-released. It's very nefarious – all this – and it might make people feel a little gloomy. But information is empowering and it's not disheartening.

It's important to know these things, because there is a bright picture beyond it, but vaccines are a horrible program, and what they have done with them. They sterilize Africans by the millions, without their permission, using vaccines... to stop population there, that's a known fact.

But what they're doing to children – as you hear in the news yourself, I'm sure, that babies are dying. They're getting multiple vaccines just after birth, they die, and then they take the mother and put her in prison for battered baby syndrome, and they don't even do an autopsy. Just to cover up the fact of what's going on. It's become that draconian and that extreme now, and people really need to wake up to it. But what they're doing instead is that they are making vaccines mandatory, which is absolutely fascist.

What are GMOs?

GMO's are genetically modified organisms. The excuse for them in plants is that these large corporations like Monsanto, have done this in order to sell their strongest, most toxic herbicide to farmers, to spray as much as they want to on the plant. But the plant has been changed, so it doesn't react to that particular poison, whereas all the other weeds do react to it and insects. So it kills everything but the plant. That sounds very smart. You know it was touted as a great advance in science when it was first pushed through by George Herbert Walker Bush, who blessed this program and got it going.

And he's been involved, as you know, in just about every horrific program going. But the genetic modification... what happens is they've even passed laws that protect Monsanto now, because the plants will cross-fertilize to somebody else who's not GMO and once the new plants become GMO, then Monsanto claims that those are their plants.

Not only that, the farmers who are harvesting these plants, they have to buy new seeds every year. They cannot use their own seeds. They are forced to buy, by law, a new round of seeds every year. They're called terminator seeds, and rightly so, which is complete... again, this is a fascist... you know... Machiavellian control of our food supply... which again, you can read that in the writings of these so-called great thinkers. So they pass these laws to protect these corporations from lawsuits, which there have been very many, from very irate farmers.

If you put a rat next to corn that is GMO and corn that is not GMO, it will not touch the GMO corn. Animals know better. They will not eat it. If they do eat it, they'll get sick and die. It's the same with cows. The cows were grazing on the leftovers of the corn in India, and the cows were dying. That's another reason the farmers were so distraught.

It's been proven in laboratories, of course. The people that are supposed to test the safety of these chemicals and the genetic modifications are the very same companies that are producing them, and this is well known, as well. It's called the revolving door of leadership. You'll see the same people in the top of Monsanto, then they'll be the head of the FDA – the federal Drug Administration – and the United States is supposed to be in charge of ensuring everybody's food safety. But it's the same people.

So you know, I'm painting a dark picture here. But it really is the reality that people need to be aware of, and as they look around, they will start to see the pattern, and well beyond all, there's a lot of empowerment to be had. So there is a silver lining to all this.

Do chemtrails exist, and if so, how would you describe them?

Yes, and there are other people who also call them aerosols or geoengineering. Aerosols – they exist, they've been – anybody who looks outside will see a crisscrossed sky, or these long lines behind jets – the new turbofan jets – a contrail which people often say, "...that's what those are, those are just water vapour," which is what a contrail is.

It's condensed water that forms ice crystals behind the jets, and I've seen those behind very high jets, military jets, since I was a kid. But they only lasted a few lengths of the plane behind it and they just dissipated as it went along.

Today, they'll stay up there all day and you can watch them spread out, and they'll take all kinds of shapes and forms in their later stages. Some people don't realize it being chemtrails, because they may change shape after they've been out for an hour or two, and they eventually cover the sky. They collect water vapour, too, so they start cute little circles, pure like a real cloud, but you can tell through the sunshine, so you'll see sort of a weird rainbow-looking effect. Well, those are the chemicals in the chemtrails.

But these do exist, they've been documented, and they've been proven, and it's one of the biggest, strangest so-called conspiracies out there. Because they keep denying that there's such a thing that exists – which is like telling you that you don't have a nose on your face – it's just insane.

But meantime they're talking about 'we're thinking of doing this,' so they often do this – they sort of prepare you for what's already going on – like it's happening in the news all the time.

We read about nanotechnology: "Oh, they found out we got nanotech dust that can affect your thinking."

Well, that's been out for a long time, but that just means that they're conditioning people to accept that reality, similar to what they're doing with chemtrails. Chemtrails, too, are carriers of nanotechnology, very small things that we're inhaling that are affecting our nervous system, and it's a very serious thing to be aware of.

I advise anybody who takes this seriously to do a detox regimen regularly. I use something called Zetox in my water regularly. But there are different powders... eating a lot of powerful, rich green nutrients is very important. But please research this for yourself, because you need to be aware of it.

One of the websites that I regularly visit is *www.geoengineeringwatch.org* and Dane Wigington is a personal friend, and he's one of the most remarkably courageous and committed activists – fighting for humanity and his very existence – that I know, and he's spoken to top-level people in government, and they've admitted that they're there, and they said, "Yes, but we can't talk about. We will lose our job."

He's been told that upfront, and that we've known all along, because that's how they keep people in check. If they start to say something like... if someone blows the whistle on vaccines, you'll see, all of a sudden he loses his job, and he's been ridiculed, he just about loses all of its benefits and everything.

So, they do it by intimidation and force. But thankfully there's a lot of whistleblowers who are telling the truth and the word is getting out, which is a wonderful thing. I hope a lot more people will join us, because people need to realize this is true and they have this validated for them... because they need to be standing on a real firm foundation of truth when they turn to do what they can to stop this insanity.

Please share your thoughts about the environment and the current weather conditions.

Well, this ties in well with the chemtrail phenomenon, because one of the stated purposes of this is weather modification. And you know there's always this big debate about global warming. Now they've changed it to climate change which is very convenient. Has the climate ever stopped changing, for goodness sake? They're attempting and succeeding at directing the jet stream via these chemtrails.

What they have is aluminium sulfate, barium sulfate, and several heavy metals that actually react to electromagnetic frequency pulses. And these are sent out via large installations, larger arrays, such as HAARP the famous one up in Alaska.

But there's about fifteen of those types of arrays around the world, on every continent, that are involved in this program, which shows you that there's an international aspect to of all of this.

While we are being given the picture that there is nation versus nation, it's actually something much bigger behind all this. But they are actually able to direct the jet stream now, because those particles react to the electromagnetic pulsing. And what they do, they bounce it off the ionosphere, which amplifies it, and it comes down much stronger, but they are also doing it from land-based radar systems. Call it radar, but they're electromagnetic antenna arrays, even single ones.

You see these big balls out in the ocean? Those are part of the program, those big white balls. You see them on top of mountains. But even beyond cell phone towers, you see this whole different array of types of antenna, and they call them heaters on the tops of these towers, and they have different purposes. So we don't know exactly what they're up to, but we know it's no good, and we know its super bad for human health.

But manipulating the weather is what's causing all this insanity. We're more dependent on the solar cycle than anything else. And if you want to explain any overall trends that seem to be the more natural ones they are realizing, well, these are some of the cause, but they don't want that... they want to blame humanity.

They want to charge money for carbon emissions. It's just insane, and carbon dioxide is one of the most essential things for earth's existence. And they're claiming it's a pollutant now, just to show how upside down everything is.

But changing the weather... they've successfully brought a drought into California. If you watch certain websites, they have unfiltered radar of the clouds there and the streams... you can see how it's been directed unnaturally right up the coast... all the moisture goes up and over and that's why the heavy deluges in the middle of the United States, because all that moisture is being directed there and then dropped.

So just like it was extremely cold on the East Coast thess past two winters, they actually can bend the arctic air down. They call this some kind of strange term, this oddly persistent loop or something, they needed to try and explain it away. But these have been directed and this has been proven by many researchers, and makes total sense.

Well, at the same time humanity is being blamed for the problem and more controls are being put into place. So this is just another way that they're coming at us. So the list is pretty massive, and again, it can seem overwhelming. But it's not, we're here for a purpose and we're here, we're alive and kicking. They haven't gotten us. They can't stop us. We are infinite consciousness and eternal beings, so we are what they fear... so, hence this big bombardment from every side on humans. But they can't stop us.

Do you have a practice that keeps your spirits high?

My main one is what I do: my researching and writing. When I write, it's a form of meditation for me, because I'm processing not just the information, but I'm sensing what's around me and what I am in and what I am, and what I've learned over the years – and I think this is important for people to also grasp at some point.

When you're going through things, people tend to blame themselves for it. "What's wrong with me?" ... that I'm depressed or I've –

you know – I'm suffering from this mistake I made or my past Karma and blah, blah, blah. Really, we've very sensitive antenna, and we pick up what's going on around us. So people learn to look outside for what they're sensing.

You realize that we're pretty much in a sea. If you look at the seaweed, they're sort of swaying in the ocean. It's a product of its environment and we're a product of this environment, not just physically, but spiritually.

There's a lot going on around us, but when you become aware of that, the sensation and the energy and the strength to connect to the ultimate source beyond all that, it's been enhanced. And that's where we derive our power. We're like solar panel arrays spiritually. We're picking up all this stuff.

Now it gets blocked, it gets filtered, and it gets manipulated just like in the physical. But when we become alive spiritually, our spirits naturally reach out and long for the true source, the real pure light, and it'll connect... just like if you watch a plant growing on fast-forward motion on a video, you'll see it come out of the ground and the leaves come up and they spread out and it catches the sunlight.

That's what the human spirit does all the time... it's looking for that, and when you become aware of that, it's wonderful.

I mean meditation is a wonderful practice, and I do my own form. I spend half an hour to an hour. I don't follow any particular regimen. I do that, also. It depends on what my circumstances are, and what's going on, but I spend a lot of time alone. I don't even listen to music – I live in a very quiet atmosphere, and I love it that way – where I can feel, and I can think, and I can create, and I can feel alive. And the beautiful view from where I sit... I go out on our porch and I look down at the ocean. I love nature, I go for long walks.

But its part of keeping a balanced life, I think, that helps that sort of plant life I'm talking about – you know – our spiritual seedling to come out. I mean, a lot of people are still on the earth, wondering what the heck is going on... "You're telling me I'm a plant? I feel like a dead seed."

But guess what, seeds germinate, and with a little bit of water, little bit of warmth, and next thing you know, wham!... you come out into the light. And that shocks people when they all of a sudden come out in the light. Their eyes hurt, like, "Where am I?" It's like a fish in water coming out of the water going, "What is this place?" It's very much like that.

But that's more or less my spiritual regimen, is pretty much my way of life which I'm very happy with, and it's taken me a long time to arrive here. But I don't care what I went through to get here. I'm happy about it and my life hasn't been easy, as most people's lives haven't.

I've have been through a lot of trauma, I've been through a lot of personal spiritual agony. I think that's awesome, that downplay people think about the physical agony and the handicaps of people, what they have to face through life. But spiritual handicaps and being spiritually browbeaten or spiritually abused, is endemic in society and in religion. People are just pounded on spiritually, but that's not addressed often enough, and that is the most devastating thing to the human spirit.

When I see the madness around me, I feel hopeless. Can you suggest some ways that would help me regain my trust in the future and how to act to make a positive change?

I say, get active. As you're learning about what's going on, share it. And interact with other people. It's really important to bring these things to light. You'll face ridicule and you'll face naysayers and all the rest, but that also helps you get over your self image, because that's what holds people back so much. They want to be part of a certain way, and they think they're supposed to act a certain way, or they're not being their old selves... people make fun of them.

Well, in some cases, change your friends, if that's the case, or change your location. But the most important thing is let yourself change organically, and that's what's happening, but by sharing with other people, and getting it out even online.

My quote on my website today is – I forget where I read it and so I put it as anonymous – but it says: "It only takes a few moments to share an article, but the person on the other end who reads it might have his life changed forever."

And that goes for anything, it could be a hug or a smile, it could be a thank you. It could be anything. But we live our lives... the love just starts coming out, and you can't help it. Because love takes action, you know, they say, "Pity feels it, but compassion takes action."

So sharing information, I think, is really important. Start a website, write, do music, be an artist, create. Get involved in your community activities or start your own activity.

I talk to people at the checkout stand all the time and talk to people in the elevators, even just to break the ice and get the ball rolling. I'll drop a little bit about this or that, and I've found a way to people in the most obscure places, just by putting a little feeler out. I make a little comment about the banks or some little comment anybody can agree on. You can tell by their response. If you're like some people, who just go, "Yeah man, I can't take this anymore," and then you got a big conversation, and it happens like that. If one person talks to two people, and two people talking to four, we're talking eight... the whole world would be covered in a matter of days by a mathematical progression.

So it's really a question of uncorking and living that life. Really find each other, I think, that's the most empowering thing when you find people of like mind.

If you could plant one seed in the mainstream mind, what would that be?

Wow, good question, one seed. I would say; *Question everything.*

Zen Gardner

One of Zen's many insightful poems:

You Can Lead a Horse to Water

You can lead a horse to water but you can't make it drink
You can give folks information but you can't make 'em think
You can put it in a wrapper or you can tie it in a bow
But if people aren't hungry they will never learn to know.

At least we put it out there where just anyone can see
So that those who might be looking can simply use it to get free
Too long these truths were hidden, not available to all
Now at least it's out there to feed the ones who hear the call

So let the truth out freely, while some may scorn or mock
('like reality is toxic, though faint and parched they walk..)
One day they'll stop and try it, whatever it may take
They'll be glad you put it out there and a better world we'll make

Ideas and words are power but the hearer must desire
To draw with will and wonder from the well of ice and fire
We cannot force or overwhelm, imposing wills on those
Who need to learn to want to choose, and so their spirit grows

But when these people activate their true imagination
They'll find the power waiting that they're One with all Creation
Knowledge is a wondrous tool yet often overblown
But mixed with love and wisdom it can really hold its own

The key is how we take it, yet it needs to be displayed
Where all can find and use it, that's how the game is played
So keep the juices flowing, no matter what the fate
Your truth and kindness waters those escaping out the gate.

In the age of information

Ignorance is a choice

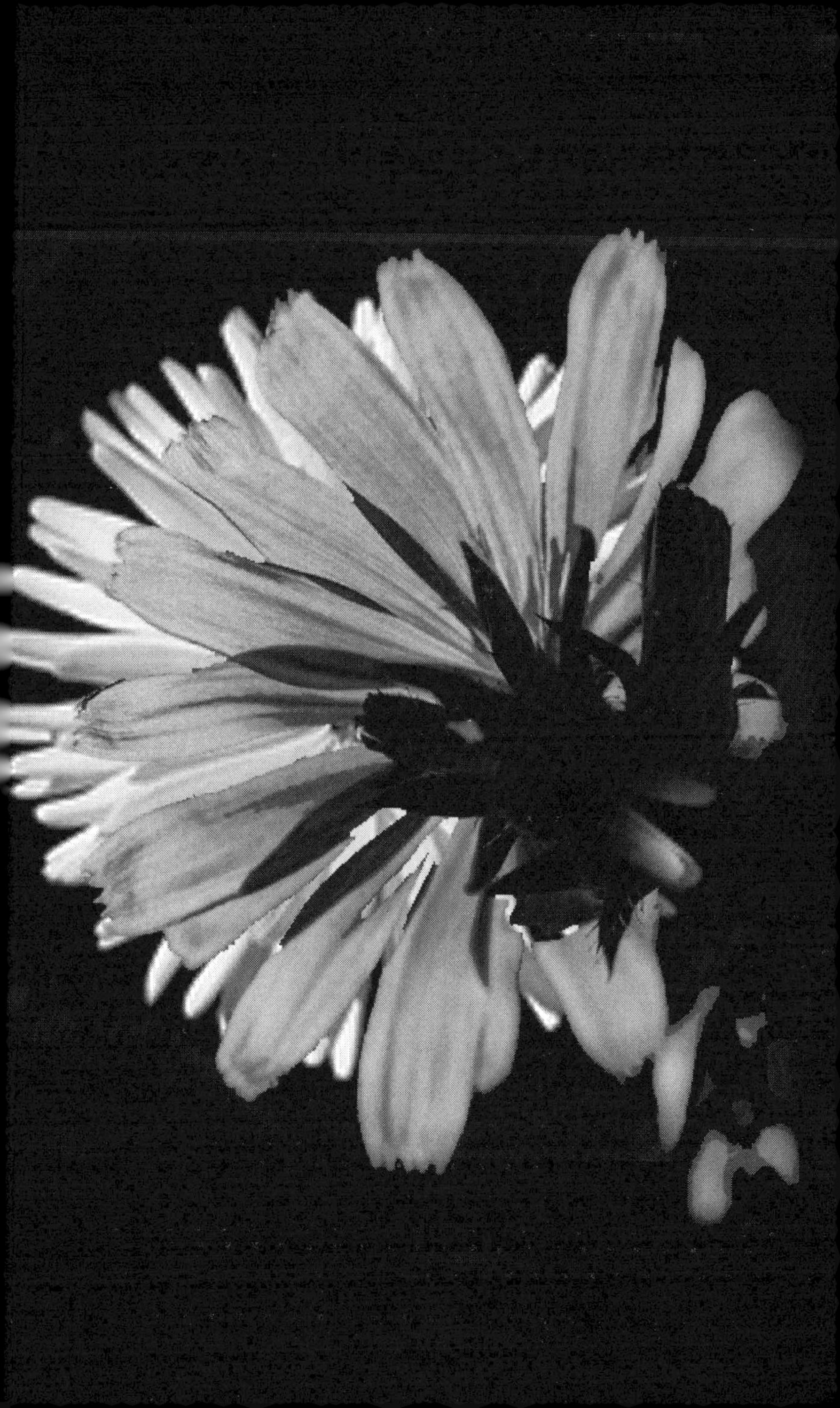

CYNTHIA McKINNEY

Cynthia McKinney

CYNTHIA McKINNEY

Introduction

Cynthia McKinney has become an internationally renowned human rights activist because of her readiness to step into the line of fire to achieve her goals.

Cynthia exposed corruption in Washington, DC and did not hesitate to hold position holders accountable. Her questioning of Donald Rumsfeld on fiscal responsibility and the tragic events of September 11th has become legendary.

Cynthia believes the public has a right to know what its government does in its name using its tax dollars. She has been stranded in international waters and rescued by the Lebanese Navy as she attempted to deliver humanitarian assistance to the besieged people of Gaza during Operation Cast Lead, Israel's 22-day military attack on Gaza, Palestine.

Also as a result of her activism around Israeli/Palestinian issues, she served seven days in an Israeli prison for attempting to deliver school supplies to Gaza's children in the aftermath of Operation Cast Lead.

> *In the fight against injustice, we stand together, and we must.*
> *In the fight against intimidation, we stand together, and we must.*
> *After all, a regime that would steal an election right before our very eyes will do anything to all of us."*
>
> – Cynthia McKinney

www.allthingscynthiamckinney.com

Cynthia, when did you start exploring your field? Was there a specific event that led you to this path of waking up?

Well, that's a very interesting question, because I don't know that I actually have a field. But I have a very curious mind, so I tend to just go as far down the rabbit hole as my time and resources will allow me to do. One of the rabbit holes that I've gone down in particular is US policy.

I have a name for it now, because of my relationship with Dr. Peter Dale Scott, who served on my dissertation committee. He has done a lifetime of research around what he calls the deep state of the US. These are the unseen hidden hands that move US policy, using US military, diplomatic, and domestic policy where no one sees what's going on.

So if anything, I could say that if I have a field, it would be the ways in which the deep state operates, to the extent that our democratic rights or the democracy that the idealized democratic US is inhibited in some way. Because of the presence of these unseen hidden forces, those are really the movers and shakers of US policy.

How do you see the world today in terms of the challenges facing us?

The situation is extremely bleak and dire. There's a group of people around the world who individually, or as parts of their own smaller circles, have done everything that one could imagine to begin to address the challenges that are facing us as humankind. And also that challenges us in terms of sustainable living and the ability of the planet to nurture us. These are just some of the challenges that are facing us.

We are challenged on every front, whether it is with the prospect of being overrun by fake organisms that have been created in a test tube, then that we are supposed to consume as nourishment. Everything that the planet has to offer to humankind has been squandered by a few. And there appears to be a philosophy that sadly is rooted in European history of plunder, predation, and populism. If it is negative, you name it, and it happens there. And it's that attitude that has been taken around the world. That's why the challenge is global.

People are struggling with how they look, because they've been called black dogs, called all kinds of things to denigrate themselves to serve as some mark of superiority. And we're dealing on that base level, as opposed to being able to deal with the level of humanity that interacts with the planet, interacts with the universe, the stars that recognize that we are celestial beings. That is a whole different way of thinking and looking at things that it's been completely lost. Because there are some people who are committed to killing the planet, and they're doing a darn good job of it, and killing humanity in the process.

Does it matter if we vote or not?

Well, I think it matters if we vote, even if the manner in which it is done is very limited. That limited amount is still important as far as I'm concerned. And so I would never recommend someone failing to vote or passing up an election. And not only should we vote at every election, but we should vote the entire ballot of every election. We just need to participate at the highest intensity that we can. For some people it is just voting. For other people it's being deep down in the process, ensuring that our elections have transparency and integrity. For other people it's supporting protesters who act as a check on a runaway system that has forgotten our value to it.

For others it could be actually running for office which is what I recommend. I recommend that average, ordinary folks run for office.

And be able to imprint their values on the system and not be changed by the system. Rather, we should change the system, rather than being changed by the system.

What are your thoughts about money and the global banks?

This is an area that is relatively new to me. I read Ellen Brown's book, and I really couldn't put it down. It became like a bible to me, because it was chock full of information. So then I became interested in the whole central bank struggle, the struggle in the United States.

Whether or not the United States is going to have a central bank and the kind of, well, I shouldn't say whether or not, the kind of central bank the United States was going to have, whether it was going to be public or private. The extent to which private individuals got together and literally manipulated the political process, which is something that continues today. Which is why the United States has become a killing machine, rather than a life-producing machine. Or as some of the Venezuelans talk to me as I was interviewing them for my dissertation... which was on the leadership of Hugo Chavez... they talked about technologies of life and technologies of death.

The United States, the entire political apparatus of the United States, is essentially a technology of death. This is something that has been allowed to happen by the people of the United States, because they failed to fight back. When, in the counterintelligence program, documents of the Federal Bureau of Investigation of United States government, write that they are going to misdirect, mislead or otherwise neutralize organizations and individuals who have the power to explain to the people of the United States, the value system that is in place, and the value system that they would like to see in place, then we understand how grave the situation has become.

Because these people have totally thoroughly misled, misdirected, and misinformed the people of the United States, whose taxpaying dollars are used to implement this policy that actually works against them.

What do you think about the debt-based economy in which people are stuck, and is there a way out?

I went from Ellen Brown to Anthony Sattin, and The Creature from Jekyll Island, and economist Michael Hudson. So I just began this foray. There's a video, The Secret of Oz, and these sources are jam-packed with information about the private central bank process and how that process is actually the opposite of what people want to have their interest in promoting prosperity for all. You can't do it with a private banking system, and you can't do it based on private debt.

My son has actually become involved in the time-banking alternative currency movement. So in his way, his contribution is that he does events and there is not a dollar that is being exchanged. But everyone brings something, and everyone leaves with something, if they choose to. And there is no US dollar exchange.

The sanctions regime has been enforced on what I call the rogue countries of the world – that is those countries that have respect for severity and the Europeans as a whole has not done that. It's been amazing to me that the big bad Europeans that have been going around the world colonising people and genocide people and trafficking people for the purpose of slavery have themselves now become slaves of the debt-based economy and not a single shoot was fired.

So anyway certainly it is not a way for prosperity for all.

We have started to read and hear about microchipping people. What does that mean?

There are many different ways of micro-chipping people. And I'm a Trekkie, I love Star Trek. I recognised very long ago that certain organisations like the new operators of the United States. Because the chairs on the deck of the Titanic, or the people occupying those chairs, are changing. So at one point the oligarchs were one set of people. Now the oligarchs are a different set of people. I don't mean just because a generational or the passage of time that the interest in the values of the oligarchs are quite different than the old oligarchs.

We also have to centralize the role of Zionism in the struggle for international dignity and justice, and understand the role, the design is a play today in the deep state aspects of US policy, and the killing machine that the United States has become.

So there are many different ways to microchip people. You don't have to put a device inside of them to control them. If you can control them with propaganda through the media, then that's easier and a cheaper way to do it. But some people have not been satisfied with that. There is the singularity movement which looks at combining artificial intelligence with individuals, thereby denying the individual will of people.

So I go back to my Star Trek example of the Borg. I see the Borg operating on many different levels of many different aspects, already operating without the actual device having been put inside a person.

So the question is how many of us can become Seven of Nine. Seven of Nine tried desperately to create a disjuncture or to disconnect herself from the Borg. So that is also a part, because we're so thoroughly immersed in the matrix, the matrix of someone else's reality that is not reflective of our own reality. And we live a reality that bears no resemblance to... .

For example, the organizers of the deep state say that the United States' economy is growing, yet everybody is poor. So people will say, "Oh well, you know," – especially because they're so desperate to support President Obama in the current day that they'll say – "Oh well, he made the economy grow," even though they're losing their jobs or they've already lost their jobs, they've lost their 4x4, they'd lost everything. But you know, the economy is growing.

People are living in this matrix of a lie that is the propaganda, the misdirection. And this is all purposeful, because it's in the COINTELPRO document that we're going to do that. Then in the Pentagon we have an entire department now that is dedicated to perception management. From the Frank Church Committee reports we understand that the CIA violated its charter in operating inside the United States with the purpose of trying to mislead and misdirect, or as the CIA called it, the grand Wurlitzer, utilizing the press to send out false messages.

To the extent that people believe those false messages, they've been micro-chipped without a device, and so that means that it takes extra effort from us to understand our condition, first of all, then to disconnect ourselves from this micro-chipping scheme.

One of the things that I recognized, when I ran for president of the Green Party ticket in 2008, was that every house that I visited – I could only stay in homes, I couldn't stay in hotels we didn't have that kind of money – it was really good that I stayed in people's homes, because what I began to see quite clearly was that the smartest people who really understood what the heck was going on were the ones who didn't have televisions. They didn't have television, so it was then easy for me to disconnect.

I disconnected myself and began to consider. And of course the Ph. D. process taught me how to evaluate. I had some notion before, but it's very clear now, after going through that process, that the system is the way it is because the people who have the power want it that way. And this is a system that has winners and losers, and we have to identify who the winners are and we have to identify who the losers are.

Now that's a very painful process. Not for me because I'm the descendant of the people who were trafficked into slave trade. So I understand what happened and what certain segments of the population are capable of.

But then there are people who actually believe, for example, that the United States government was always going to be there for them. They really believed that there's apple pie and that every person has a home, the justice system. They believed everything is true, because of white supremacy, that there was a period when the United States government did work for them. But now the noose is even being tightened around the body politic of the necks of those who founded the country.

So we have to understand that there are many different ways in which we have been collectively micro-chipped, and we have to struggle to disconnect ourselves from that.

What are your thoughts about depopulation?

Oh well, that's not a secret, of course, everyone understands that part of the objective is to kill people. And if you can get the people that you don't like to kill each other, then that's so much for the better. And that's been going on ever since the colonized world began to wake up to the pernicious effect on them of the whole colonial process.

So it is not an accident that those who are the most vociferous voices in the overpopulation crowd are the very people who were the ones who benefited from centuries of colonial activity.

What is your opinion on vaccines? And is vaccination part of the depopulation question?

Well, what you allow to be done to others is going to come back and be done to you. So that it the situation with vaccines. People remained silent when the syphilis study was being done by the United States government on black men in Tuskegee, Alabama. Now we've recently discovered that they did the same thing to innocent people in Guatemala.

So this killing machine is operating on all fronts. You don't have to be blown up or eviscerated by a drone attack to become subject to depopulation. And of course you have the whole Planned Parenthood issue that I'm investigating now because of the recent revelations with the videos, the heinous videos, and the facts, as put to me, that Planned Parenthood comes out of the eugenics movement. So what if the values of the eugenics movement constitute the current values today of the organisation that receives many millions of dollars of tax payers money, that is known as Planned Parenthood?

So the vaccines are only a part of it. There are the Georgia Guidestones that I have not visited, but I've seen pictures of. My goal when I go back to Georgia… I want drive up there and see the Georgia Guidestones and see for myself if they really exist, first of all.

Secondly, if the cornerstone has been replaced with a cornerstone that says 2015. If it has, then that is significant. I would say that is significant. I don't trust the United States government in any aspect of the United State government as far as I could throw it.

What are GMOs?

Genetically modified organisms that demonstrate the capability of science to match tomatoes with fish, to match humans with mice. I mean it's just test tubing everything, test tubing life. These people think that they can do that and they're in the process of actually doing it. It's technology of death.

So what I would advise people is don't eat anything… certainly don't eat anything that's processed in the United States, because you can't trust it. You can't trust it one bit.

When the Federal Drug Administration of the United States government, which has jurisdiction over approving certain foods for being put on the market, approved cloned meat and cloned fish for people to consume, you know that this is not something that you want to have any part of, with the GMO foods, even down to GMO chocolate.

This is a technology death, because that stuff is not alive. And if it came from a test tube, it's not alive. I'm against all of it, including, at one point, having advised soldiers in the United States government not to take those vaccines, to abstain, because what I discovered when I was in the US Congress is that the corporations that won the contracts to administer didn't deserve it and didn't have the expertise.

So those contracts were awarded on the basis of insider sweetheart deals that had nothing to do with the helping the soldiers. In fact the United States government doesn't care one whit about the health of their soldiers or their better ends, for that matter, because we can see it in the way they actually treat them.

Do chemtrails exist, and if so, how would you describe them?

Well, chemtrails are those fake clouds that are up in the sky. At one point they used to be extremely prevalent. You could see them actually, you could see them as they were being made and eventually they dispersed throughout the sky and created a kind of haze. And people just think, "Oh, it's a hazy day." But it's something else which independent individuals, who are not necessarily even scientists, have stepped up in to a leadership role and said, "Okay, let me take samples of what's falling down and eventually reaching my soil."

And what they found was increased rates of aluminum. Other people who do have a background have been able to test the materials. I had a conversation with a nurse who told me that she was able to get the material collected. She had a whole list of a cocktail menu of some radioactive, some not radioactive, ingredients that have been put in the sky that we all breathe.

We've not been told by our government what the purpose of this geo-engineering, as it's now called.

But the Italians have done a fantastic investigation that they turned into a documentary. And in that documentary the Italians do have some credibility with me personally, because they expose the whole Operation Gladio through their anti-terrorism operation of their government. They exposed... I think it is Guido Savini... I think that was his name. He was a judge and he was charged with investigating a series of bombings that went all the way back. He went all the way down into the rabbit hole and discovered that at the end of the day it was an operation that was carried out by the United States CIA, with their allies in the various European countries.

This was an effort to contain the left-leaning politics, particularly the Italians, the Greeks, and the Spaniards, who generally would be a little bit more left-leaning. It was called Operation Gladio. So the Italians exposed that and they did this investigation on geo-engineering or chem-trails, and what they discovered was that the particles actually serve as a desiccating function to allow the deeper penetration of the US military intelligence apparatus, like the NSA, other listening devices, listening programs, and organizations to function more properly. But ultimately a military and an anti-privacy purpose was being served by this geo-engineering and chemtrails.

Please share your thoughts about the environment and the current weather conditions.

Well, I'm a greenie, what they call a tree hugger – I'm proud of it – tree hugger and proud.

So the current weather conditions do concern me, but I've only begun to look at the condition, the planetary conditions of weather. But also what I've come to understand is that's space weather, because we are a part of something much larger. So this is what ancient Mayans understood.

Ancient man was at least smart enough without all of the technological scientific advancement that we hail in the twenty-first century. They were at least able to understand that we are part of the earth. The earth is a part of the universe, the earth and the sun and the moon are all a part of us and that we are affected by these larger forces. As we can affect planetary forces, so there is this continuum and we have to understand and recognize that. Some people never forgot that, and hence the effort to control these forces, which is stupid.

But if you have this idea that you yourself constitute a mini-God, and you have the power of life and death in your hands, then, of course, you not only feel that way, but act in that way, not just toward yourself, but toward other people. Everything has a limit. These people don't stop with their technologies of death.

Do you have a practice that keeps your spirits high?

No, I probably need to get one. But it just seems like I'm crushed with the weight of... there is so much to do.

There is a dissertation that I want to read from my institution in Antioch University, and the name of it is: What Keeps Them Going? Because that ultimately is what I would use to make sure that my spirits are high. I haven't done it yet. I haven't even downloaded it. I need to go to the Website of Antioch University and download it, *What Keeps Them Going?*

The researcher looked at lives of activist women who have dedicated their whole lives to activism. They didn't stop, they just kept going. So that would be something that I think would be very, very interesting to me.

Perhaps this interview will spur me to go ahead and download it and read it, so I can share the information with others of us who understand that we need to keep going.

And we know we need to keep going. We get tired and not to give in to being tired, like Fannie Lou Hamer said, "I'm sick and tired of being sick and tired," and figure out a way to keep our spirits high so that we can continue to move and act in accordance with our sick-and-tiredness.

When I see the madness around me, I feel hopeless. Can you suggest some ways that would help me regain my trust in the future and how to act to make a positive change?

If you look up at night, and you look at the stars, you look at the sky.

I remember when I was on a boat with a bunch of other activists and the Israelis were harassing us as we were trying to get to Gaza. The Israelis were harassing us and they introduced this new kind of machine we've never seen before... I never even heard of... it's probably part of some secret military arsenal that was handed to them by the US. It's a wave-making machine.

So basically what the Israelis did was, we're out in the middle of the Mediterranean and have two-thirds of the way to Gaza still in international waters. And the Israelis start trailing us, and then they deploy this machine after they disconnected the GPS. So they jam the GPS signals, so we had no way of knowing of where we were.

Then they deployed this wave-making machine... and it was just a little ferry... it wasn't even a boat... so it could easily have tipped over. They created these huge, huge waves and the purpose of this harassment was to get us to inadvertently go into Israeli territory or waters, so they would have an excuse to board us and do whatever.

And that scheme didn't work, so I asked the captain, because there was a whole mess going on. So the captain said we never once went into Israeli waters, because he used the stars and the moon to navigate.

That just reminded me who we really are. I mean we are like the Egyptians and all of those ancient people who looked up at the sky. They had far more knowledge about the planet, about Earth, about living. They had far more than we have, because through "civilization" we've been removed from that.

So that one instance reminded me, look up into that sky and understand my relationship with the sky. So it's not just the skies in the daytime vast... the geo-engineering, and the chemtrails, and the weather modification, and the other stuff that goes on, but the skies might help us restore our humanity... and if anything, that is what gives me hope for the future.

When I see a flower blooming, it's real. My son does urban agriculture, he grows food, and he uses composting. So he has understood that cycle of life and our connectedness. He works with farmers to understand our connectedness with planting certain crops, certain times, based on the lunar cycle.

These are things that we've completely lost in the rush for a questionable civilization.

If you could plant one seed in the mainstream mind, what would that be?

Question everything. Especially question those who are in authority today. Question their decisions and demand accountability and transparency.

Made in the USA
Lexington, KY
15 November 2018